8,08

Essay Index

RENAISSANCE IN THE NORTH

BY
W. GORE ALLEN

Essay Index

Essay Index Reprint Series

 BOOKS FOR LIBRARIES PRESS
FREEPORT, NEW YORK

Renaissance in the North by W. Gore Allen
First Published 1946 by Sheed and Ward, Inc., New York

Reprinted 1970 by arrangement.

STANDARD BOOK NUMBER:
8369-1590-9

LIBRARY OF CONGRESS CATALOG CARD NUMBER:
79-111810

PRINTED IN THE UNITED STATES OF AMERICA

South of the river stood Saint Olav's Church . . .
and thither they must go to mass to-morrow. . . .
In former days, when the Norwegians sailed their
own merchandise to London town, this had been
their church.

SIGRID UNDSET, *The Master of Hestviken*.

A NOTE TO PURISTS

THE writer is aware that in the Scandinavian languages vowels should occasionally be modified with a circled *umlaut*, and that 'ø' is a separate letter. Owing to general difficulties of production, these facts have sometimes been ignored.

ACKNOWLEDGMENT

THE following material was the basis of ten lectures, delivered for the Workers' Educational Association. This Association is hereby thanked for its kind permission to reproduce the material in its present form.

CONTENTS

PAGE

THE BACKGROUND 9

THE CATHOLIC 37
Sigrid Undset—Medieval.
Sigrid Undset—Modern.

THE PROTESTANTS 60
Sóren Kierkegaard.
Selma Lagerlöf.

THE AGNOSTIC 87
J. P. Jacobsen.

THE NATIONALISTS 101
Verner von Heidenstam.
Knut Hamsun.

THE INFLUENCE OF MUSIC 129
Grieg and Sibelius.

INDEX OF PERSONS 141

LIST OF ILLUSTRATIONS

HENRIK IBSEN   *Frontispiece*
By courtesy of Royal Norwegian Information Services

FACING FACE

SIGRID UNDSET 36
By courtesy of Royal Norwegian Information Services

SÓREN KIERKEGAARD 60

SELMA LAGERLÖF 72
By courtesy of Bertil Norberg, Stockholm

J. P. JACOBSEN 88
By courtesy of the Royal Danish Government

VERNER VON HEIDENSTAM 102
By courtesy of the Swedish-British Society

EDVARD GRIEG 130
By courtesy of the Royal Norwegian Information Services

JAN SIBELIUS 134
By courtesy of Ivar Helander, Helsinka-Helsingfors

THE BACKGROUND

THE following lectures were delivered, both in response to a demand and also to counteract, within the limitations of a small provincial class, the most striking tendency of extra-mural teaching in our times. The demand was for a 'literary subject'. The ground to be covered must not be English ground, since it was felt that the novelists from Thackeray to Hardy, from Wells to Graham Greene, had been masticated with such Gladstonian reverence that there was nothing left to chew. Nor, since the responsible association was striving to avoid controversy at almost any cost, could it be Russian, German, Spanish, American, or Japanese. The suggestion to study some modern Scandinavian writers was welcomed with relief.

Because the promotion of all learning, outside the universities themselves, has been shouldered by those who were once Liberal-Nonconformist and are now Socialist-Agnostic, we cannot grumble when we discern their special bias. Inheriting characteristics through the blood and breathing them in daily with fresh air, men strive in vain to be impartial. In any case, the average class knows after twenty minutes the politics and religion, if any, of its tutor. His best plan is probably to confess at once.

With the exception of a course on music, the lectures running parallel with these were concerned with Psychology and the Geographical Problems of the Danube. Both gave the German Schoolmaster (enemy of Europe, arch-enemy of culture) ample opportunity to elaborate his thesis. That he used instruments who would have recoiled in horror from their task had they noticed him behind them, did not make the bias less effective. A strong antidote was urgently required.

II

A teacher learns soon enough to practise guile. To have said in the present case that a second spring of Christian faith was manifest throughout the modern literature of Scandinavia would have prepared the lectures for a deaf reception. Such an idea must be approached obliquely. Even so, mere arrangement of material gave away the game. The class was told that it was to study Sigrid Undset as a Catholic, Selma Lagerlöf and Kierkegaard as Protestants, Jacobsen as an Agnostic, and the remaining authors as Nationalists of different types. Yet this was not believed. Mental reflexes are never shaken quickly. Just as, despite every proof of sheer hardheadedness which the most prosaic Government on earth can give us, Ireland is still associated with the fantastic and unpractical, carried to their last extremes of twilight, so Scandinavia is the region which stopped dead when it had produced *A Doll's House* on the stage and the 'Middle Way' in political and social thinking. A few lectures would not shake such theories. The unhappy teacher must continue to look around for earthquakes.

But if the chief purposes of education are to broaden the mind, to deepen the spirit, and enrich the heart, the joy which it will bring must always be rooted in surprise. Teacher and pupils set out together for a kingdom. When they are studying the exact sciences, of logic, mathematics, and even the philosophy of music, this kingdom is a state which belongs entirely to the mind. It has neither landmarks nor artificial frontiers, dialects nor customs, unless these are endowed by the imagination. When, however, such a voyage is directed to a country, or a group of countries, existing geographically on maps, politically through the speeches and actions of their leading statesmen, and more personally in novels and in poems, the explorers find their feet. They will discriminate between that which is worthy of their love and of their hatred; and of course they will draw comparisons upon the smallest data. We laugh at Prince Albert, when he compared the Scottish Highlands with the mountains of Saxe-Coburg. But was this so absurd ? We are doing the same thing every day, since we have only to set foot upon a foreign shore, and we begin to muse: "This undulation is like the little hill I used to see on spring mornings from my bedroom window. This might be the river I used to fish for trout. Do you see that wood ? It might be the plantation where we played Red Indians twenty years ago. . . ." A new land is never unfamiliar. Soon enough we discover terms through which we can express it.

III

For literary purposes the Scandinavian countries should be treated always as a unit. Iceland may have been the parent of the others; Denmark may have borrowed unashamedly from Norway—as Sweden has from Finland; the fact remains that there is an historical cycle common to them all. In the Classical autumn, which was also the first of many Christian springs, they produced the Saga. During the Gothic Middle Ages they were influenced wholly by the Church; for she was developing their native gifts and also acquainting them with a wider culture. After the Reformation, Paris, and finally Berlin, became in turn their centre of attraction. The Norse were rusticated by polite society; treated so openly as unteachable barbarians that they were driven back upon their own resources. In the seventeenth century a Dano-Norwegian translation of the Bible, together with the Sagas, was the staple literature of northern Europe.

This reappearance of the Sagas had a lasting effect on Scandinavian writing. Character rather than scenery or setting, actions rather than personal motives or personal decisions, was emphasized by the classic authors; and it was accepted by the moderns as one facet of a grand, unbreakable tradition. Human character in turn possessed certain marks by which it could be recognized and measured. The chief attribute would be the will for freedom. Adventurers, travellers, explorers, the Vikings had quested far afield in search of liberty: liberty to grow, after their own kind, in physical and mental stature.

The type of society which they were capable of forming was visible in Iceland from 1100 to 1270. On the first of these two dates the descendants of those men who had escaped the despotic rule of Harold Fairhair were sufficiently ensconced to make free terms with the Norwegian Crown. Now they could insist that Canon Law be held in reverence; that special benefits be granted to the producers of agricultural wealth; that politics be organized on the basis of scattered villages and manors. By 1270, however, when Icelandic custom gave place to the new Norwegian code, this way of life had become extinct. It belonged to the twelfth century alone: a time of savage personal feuds, but a time when the Church did not compete for transitory prizes. Catholicism then could be quite simple and direct, because its fundamental nature approved the basic pattern of society. Tension between things consecrated to the service of God and things given over to the world was reduced to a minimum degree, and therefore the arts did not reflect it, as they were doing in southern Europe. When this colonial rhythm was adopted on the mainland, it had to defend itself against exterior foes rather than against destructive powers within its very nature. While the Norman cathedrals farther south were at once massive, forbidding, welcoming, and gay, the stave-churches on the mainland and the round churches on the island of Bornholm were perfect expressions of the single eye. Christians were protected by the altar as chickens are comforted and warmed beneath their mother's wing.

A literature, nourished by individual families and transmitted by their members throughout the peaceful years, was ready to battle for the faith when the faith itself was challenged by surrounding pagans. Olav was the typical protagonist of Christian ethics, just as *Heimskringla* was the mould into which, consciously or else from second nature, all future Scandinavian writing would be pressed:

It befell one Sunday when the King sat in his high-seat at table that he fell into deep thought and heeded not the hours. He had a knife in his hand and held a stick in his hand from which he was cutting shavings. A lad waiting on him stood before him holding a table dish. He saw what the King was doing, and perceived that he was thinking of other things. He said: "To-morrow is Monday, my lord." The King looked at him when he heard that, and then it struck his mind what he had been doing. He bade them bring him a lighted taper and he swept into his hand all the shavings he had cut; he set light to it and let the shavings burn in the hollow of his hand. Thereby it might be noticed that he would hold fast to God's law and commandment, and would not set aside what he knew to be right. . . .

When we contrast Olav's scruple for the last jot and tittle of the third commandment[1] with the historical knowledge—that he was a doughty warrior and a mighty pillager of cities—we see the two allurements which faced, and will always face, the Scandinavian spirit. The one was of the mind or reason, to gain inward peace on earth and external joy in heaven. The other was of the blood, unreasonable, nostalgic: to man the ships when the yearly corn was gathered, to explore a world brimming over with plunder, adventure, and the wild foray.

Goethe grasped this conflict, distilling it into a line of poetry:

> A longing pure and not to be described
> Drove me to wander over woods and fields,
> And in the midst of hot abundant tears
> I felt a world arise and live in me.

Yet Goethe, flourishing generations later, and in a province which had once been fully part of Christian Europe, could only discern it from a distance. He could not feel and know it. Weimar, and all the medieval cities, had long since found their safety-valve for this dynamic of the Northern blood. The great cathedral, the confluent lines of mighty pillars, the lighted chancel behind the hanging rood—above all, the

[1] Douay Version.

Gregorian Chant, floating down to the listeners through space:
these were at once a substitute for roving and at least a trial
at sublimation.

For the Scandinavian there was no such shelter. A baptized
Christian, he was brother to all men in the faith: a man
beyond the Holy Roman Empire, he was an unknown quantity,
a free-lance. He moved in a partial desolation; between his
life and freezing there were the rough pelts of forest creatures;
between his life and starving the coarse flesh which lay beneath
them. There in the European waste-lands he heard the voice
of God; developing, and over-developing, his conscience.
A time would come when he must strive to slay it, calling in
psychologists to condemn its every dictate. Yet it is there,
a part of him, his member. Without it, he ceases to experience
human wholeness.

IV

The study of literature leads inevitably to such a quest for
the source of national inspiration. Writers are inspired by
the peculiar circumstances of birthplace and family tradition,
but they are moved no less by the collective memory and
understanding of their people. Sometimes the historical sense
proves stronger than the personal, while at others they combine
harmoniously and even gladly. But when an alien culture is
imposed, there can be no harmony whatever. This was the
fate of Scandinavia at the Reformation, for then the far North
was conquered (so far as the intellect can yield while a spirit
battles on) by the Germans, maintaining its rebellion beneath
a deceptive layer of acquiescence. There are other ways of
conquest. It may happen, as it did in Ireland, through attrition
of such durance that both sides almost forget there is a state
of conflict. Or, a conquering army coming back to reassure
its Senate that 'Carthage is deleted', the sword may have
driven one manner of living to the shambles, while a new one
is even then being fertilized with blood. And then again,
ancient forms may wither, as gradually and imperceptibly as
summer, while young forms are ushered in around them.

It was in such a fashion that China saw the rising of the Mongols, or Imperial Rome lay sleeping, to awaken as the Holy Roman Empire.

There is a striking similarity between the fates of Scandinavian and of Irish culture. The champions of orthodox religion in the North, from Helgesen to Sigrid Undset, were reared on the Protestant and Liberal traditions. In Ireland such men as Yeats and Synge, taking their country farther back than the defensive spirit of O'Connell—to a time when the civilized world had called it a land of saints and scholars—came forth to do so from the Irish 'Middle Nation'. This layer, packed between the native peasants and the British Government-officials, was the last quarter from which an awakening was to be expected. Yet Yeats and Synge left the trim demesne behind them, going out to seek a culture which their families had hated, ridiculed, and at last ignored. They found it—on hillsides where men fought to cultivate a heap of stones; on dry patches of the bog where almost naked children wove mats from coloured grasses; over the half-doors of the cabins where old women told their beads beside the fire. It was Yeats, from a Protestant stronghold of the Middle Nation, who felt a passionate concern that the ancient way of life should be victorious:

> I write it out in a verse—
> MacDonagh and MacBride
> And Connolly and Pearse
> Now and in time to be,
> Wherever green is worn,
> Are changed, changed utterly;
> A terrible beauty is born.

And it was Sigrid Undset, returning to the spirit of her people from an alien background, who could write—not this time of merely national glory, but of a glorious Atonement:

He had heard many times that God's mercy is without bounds, and in secret he had relied on this. . . . God's arms spread out on the cross, ready to enfold him, grace streaming from the five wounds,

the drooping Head which looked down over all creation, watching
and waiting . . . the Bread of Life was ever upon the altar: God
was without bounds. . . .[1]

In these ten hundred years, between the flight of free men
from Harold Fairhair and their posterity's acknowledgment of
Sigrid Undset's claim to speak for her own people, a literary
wheel had never run full circle. Starting from the Sagas,
Catholic Christianity gave it impetus enough to move around,
through the contemplative writing of St. Bridget, towards a
point where the Church and northern Europe have always
pictured a splendid fusion of their talents. This was not to be.
The Reformation, bringing as it did Germany's intellectual
conquest of peoples from Würtemberg to Tromsö, forced the
wheel back, in self-protection, to the Sagas. Tansen wanted to
recast it—on a German axis: Helgesen, a St. Thomas More in
Denmark, achieved a conscious reversion. Only the Christian
writers of our day have been able to insist that a universal
faith was meant to be expressed through a diversity of genius.

V

Such a hurried view need not neglect the Liberal intervention;
and to clarify its place in Scandinavian letters Voltaire's epigram
may at last be useful. When Ibsen brought about an impact
between his native culture and the totality of European thought,
Europe itself was neither holy, nor Roman, nor an empire.
Since the time of organic unity the whole continent had
endured the birth-pangs, and the death-throes also, of an
artistic and philosophical Renaissance; it had been shaken
by religious heresies and bled white by the wars which they
engendered: an age of faith had given way before an age of
reason, and that again had made room for an age of high
romance. Prior to 1880 the educated public of London,
Berlin, or Washington, D.C., looked upon the North (on the
rare occasions when they did so) as a hinterland; a place, as

[1] *The Master of Hestviken.*

the Irish say, which is 'behind the back of God'. Yet after 1890 the Northern towns, and Christiania in particular, were the holies of advanced thought, experiments in living, and consequent emancipation from restraints. During this one decade, which has been called the 'Liberal Epoch', Scandinavia had come from the hem into the centre. The Western World had taught her many things, and, to its own astonishment, the Western World had learnt some things from her.

Let us understand that our use of the word 'Liberal' in this context does not suggest political or social programmes, nor does it lead us to the British Liberal Party. It is a vague term, approaching the ultra-modern 'Left'— because it begins a reflex action of the mind without the bother of a logician's connotation. After all, linen fabrics do not enrage the cliché bull; what does the trick is a suggestion of flames and blood conveyed to his senses by a strip of dyed material. Thus the word 'Left' will drive to suicide or murder any 'Rightist' in our present strange society. . . .

Confusion has to be avoided. Although the Scandinavian writers of this epoch wished, as they said, to 'let in fresh air' upon such institutions as church and home and school, at least the Norwegians of their number were loudly patriotic. While we do not doubt the essential patriotism of our Liberal statesmen, they are seldom associated in the mind with anything so gaudy as a national flag, or so strident as a national anthem. (They may not 'go out', like Chesterton's Modernists, with a 'whine': certainly they never do so with a 'shout'.) The reason for patriotism on the part of the Norwegian Liberals was that Norway had been under foreign rule—in thrall to Denmark from the Middle Ages to the Napoleonic Wars, in an unhappy union with the Swedes from 1815 to 1905.

Sweden may well be the most reactionary of European countries. There class-distinction has been reduced to a fine art; for though count's son and sweep's son share a common schoolroom, they do so with the absolute conviction that they will share nothing else until they die. Norway rebelled against

B

this atmosphere, typifying as it did all the affairs of an un-harmonious 'double nation'. The new anthem was composed by a Liberal, Björnson. *Ja, vi elsker dette landet:* Yes, in truth we love this country. . . .

The question is not so much whether Liberalism was 'right' or 'good' as whether, here and now, it can be made to serve a useful purpose. If human thought is fallible, and damnable always when carried to extremes, there is an essential dignity in man which allows the preservation of some beauty during the worst periods of his history, and a saving grace which compels him to tell at least a fraction of the truth. To the Liberals we owe the right of women to administer property independently of men, and thus their new concern for all wise administration; equitable treatment of children born outside the marriage tie; a tolerance—itself the necessary prelude to conversion—of those who hold awkward and unorthodox opinions. A hard experience has shown the North of Europe that Liberal sociology, built on a negation, fashions a whole order which is baser and much duller than the old one. Society, knowing that it needed a corrective, reached blindly for the Fascists' trim solution. This also was negative and sterile. While the Liberals taught that man required no more than freedom, the Fascists returned towards a brute creation: in their view fighting was the natural way of life and death under fire the proper way of dying. Like all heresies, this was doomed to failure from the moment of conception.

Letters, and in particular the problem-conscious literature of the last two generations, may yield up a stronger key to such a failure than the ones which are given by government Blue Books or sectional blue-prints. Home-made writing catches the homeland off its guard; a difference between the 'snap' of a small boy romping with his brother and a studio 'portrait' of the same boy in his Sunday best. Of course, we may be connoisseurs, approaching foreign letters in search of style or form or language. . . . If we are not, we can do so because our own democracy has reached a climax, and because we wish to see how others are weathering the tempest. We know that beyond this point the peoples of every European country will either govern, artisans, operatives, farm-workers taking deep and responsible decisions, or else that they will wash their hands of ruling, to leave it with a few picked men who are constitutionally remote from day-to-day experience. But if these, 'the Workers', are in fact to govern, they must increase their understanding; if they would understand, they have got to learn; if they would learn, they must choose the field of their enquiry.

Of all such grounds, the one which stretches beyond our frontiers is in most urgent need of cultivation; since what we reap from this will affect the national harvest. At peace, we may perfect the education of our children; insure that the towns shall encroach no farther on the country; protect ourselves against the scourge of unemployment. At war, these essentials become luxuries at once, to be sacrificed, along with liberty itself. Here, too, the individual counts, for when he knows the truth, propagandists cannot lie in safety, and where he has made friends it is in vain that the Devil sows his seed of hatred.

Our most pressing task is to convert the forced alliances of war into bonds which are sweeter and more lasting—mutual fear of an aggressor into amity free-chosen. Finding a hedge on one side, and a ditch upon the other, the countryman would set to work until he had made sensible gateways and reliable plank-bridges. Why not follow his example? Once agree that literature serves a purpose higher than relaxation or escape, and we shall search for literary ground on which to meet our comrades. Scandinavia, and Norway especially, is the obvious place of meeting. She lies midway, in geography, and in culture also, between the British Isles and Russia; no less effectively she can link the old world closer to the new.

The mighty protagonists of Russian culture, from the time of Kiev's greatness down to Orthodoxy's re-emergence as a suffering Church amongst the common people, have insisted that man cannot be happy until his soul is actually fused with the Creator: the Norwegian Liberals said that man would be unhappy until he was free to be himself. Two such ideas are not contradictory, and they may well be complementary. For what other meaning have the texts—"I will not call you servants . . ." "You are my friends . . ." than that we shall attain to oneness with our God when we grant ourselves the *liberty* to do so ? Again, the Americans have taught that only a full equality before the law will make a nation prosperous, while the latter-day Norwegians have claimed that there is no prosperity where the land is neglected and deep-rooted traditions are ignored. These, too, may well be complementary. Britain is pledged to establish her rural life in such a way that future blockades will fail in their intention, and she knows that the memory of past heroic stands has enabled her to face the storm of steel. A careful study, in any direction whatsoever, will provide its own answers to contemporary questions. Life is an unbroken pattern: literature confirms and underlines it.

VI

Without some biographical particulars it would be hard to estimate the exact function of these progressive writers in the life and literature of northern Europe. As it is with all men, they were mostly what circumstances made them. Ibsen, coming from one background, believed that the business of the stage was to present a host of disputations: Jonas Lie, differently reared and endowed with a different quality of genius, maintained in writing the aloofness from questions of the day which Manet and Dégas were to demonstrate on canvas.

Ibsen was born in 1828 and died in 1906—the first year of Norway's independence. His work attained its zenith with *The Wild Duck* in 1884, but his international reputation was not finally established until he was engaged upon the plays of dotage: *Little Eyolf* (1894), *John Gabriel Borkman* (1896), and *When The Dead Awaken* (1900). On the father's side he was of Scottish blood, while both parents were a mixture of the Scandinavian races, and of German. He was poor, apprenticed to a chemist, hated the work, and began to write in secret. Within a few years a theatrical company at Bergen had created a special job for him—as 'Theatre Poet'. This entailed the writing of plays, stage-management, and acting—all for the benefit of a 'business' audience. Marrying and going to live in Oslo (then called Christiania), he fought every trait of the contemporary Norwegian drama—self-satisfaction, romanticism, and the love of show. When Parliament refused him the grant to which he was entitled, he left Norway to make Italy and Germany the lands of his adoption. He was 'without honour' until he had written the words of *Peer Gynt*. It was then too late for reconciliation. His place in Norway was with the Bohème of Christiania: the opposition, the stronghold of the young against the old; of aesthetes and intellectuals against the common people.

Turn from this to the career of Jonas Lie. For Lie, Norway was a microcosm of the world. He had good cause to understand it: its geography, ethnography, and history. Born near Christiania in 1833, he left the capital while he was still a little boy, and he lived at Tromsö—a town of the midnight sun —until his thirteenth year. He enlisted in the Navy, but was dismissed his ship because a medical board had failed to notice that he had an affliction of the eyes. His eyes always gave him trouble, so that he was thrown back on super-sensual impression, or imagination. He attended schools, built specially for impoverished students, where they managed to coach him for a university degree. Meanwhile he was beguiling his companions with the wildest stories which he had learnt from friends at Tromsö. He became a 'character'; the type of man who is never taken seriously, but whose whole manner leaves its mark on other people, long after he has left them.

After the university, Lie accepted government employment as a lawyer. At that time the law seemed to be his true vocation: he could grasp the essentials of any case with speed; his moral courage was of the high order which does not shrink from tangled problems and unpopular decisions; above all, he possessed a balanced mind. He was sent to deal with 'life in the raw' upon the Swedish frontier. There, as in every border-country, men quarrelled on the smallest pretext, drank in secret, and gambled in non-existent holdings. Lie developed a 'toughness' to match the prevalent conditions, yet he lost neither his self-respect nor his reputation. Being lonely, he began to write. Memories of the far North inspired *The Visionary*, his first book; a work wholly fantastic, half traditional, in any case well beyond the range of social dramas. The support which he received, almost immediately, from Björnson meant everything to a young man, unknown, and potentially in opposition. He was fighting against the current trend of Scandinavian letters, for he was content to be a novelist, and not a social thinker or a social worker. Here he maintained the dignity and independence of his craft. *The Visionary* was scorned by men who had never seen a vision, just as his later books—sea-stories such as *The Pilot and His Wife* or *Go Ahead* —were to be derided by intelligent young fellows who had never, in their whole lives, sat on the jetty-steps and listened to a sailor. The Liberals were creating a dangerous literary ethos, and Lie was the first to war against it. He saw that the reading-public was becoming exclusively an *urban* public; that it was making a 'corner' in the arts; that it would banish from this corner all those who could not accept its arbitrary standards.

We cannot understand how arbitrary they were until we have pondered the final implications of typically Liberal thinking—as it appears, for example, in *A Doll's House*. When Nora slammed the door on home and husband, she was not running away merely from 'mutual help and protection'— the preliminary 'Beloved' and the ultimate 'Amazement'. She was deserting the common life of earth, with its experiences which are quickened and intensified in marriage: the birth of children; sharing the terrible anxiety when they are taken ill and the gasping relief when they recover from a sickness; sharing the lack of money and a sudden windfall; sharing food and drink; fine days and wet; growing old, and sharing the final awakening in death. If the poor experience these things from closer quarters, Nora was deserting them in a special manner. Her return—the treasure for which this price was paid—would be more nebulous than the ending of a rainbow: the chance that somewhere, at some vague time, kithless and alone, she might learn to be 'herself'.

It has been said of Ibsen that he was a revolutionary doomed to quarrel with every revolution, and a Christian mystic unable to find his home in any Christian communion. The first half of the sentence may be true enough: anyone who is acquainted with the mystics—from à Kempis at one end to Eckhardt at the other—will know that the second half is false. For these privileged members of the Church Militant on Earth, withdrawn and celibate themselves, have never belittled the possibilities of marriage for salvation. Indeed, to them, as to every Catholic, the family has always been the most important unit in society. Had Ibsen really been a mystic the play which he must have been called upon to write would have dealt with a young couple, prevented through the lack of money from living naturally together.

Was it pure chance that kept him from such a situation? Even then, as the Victorian age was closing, it was about to be the pith of every social question. If the Scandinavian Liberals did not face it, neither did the Liberals in France or Germany or Britain. From their abundant stock, they could spare no pity for the young couple desiring to have children. The reason is, perhaps, that their 'greatest number' was not a dynamic, but a static: the population, or the race, at any given time; not men as they are, here and now, and as they must become. In common with all heresiarchs, these Utilitarians possessed the distinguishing mark of unnaturalness. Their thesis 'went against' history, tradition, and the strongest instincts of the human heart. For, whatever men may do is done, in the last analysis, to benefit their children—whether they are defending a few acres from the bailiffs or a whole country from invasion. Speaking of the 'home-land' or the 'nation', their mind's eye is occupied with something far more humble: a cradle, and after that, a cradle.

Beyond this, the world in which such men as Brandes, Mill, and Ibsen had been cast was even then an old world. Instead of championing the rights of a younger against the privileges of an older generation, they championed the greybeards who wanted to behave like striplings. For them it was a natural folly, since it was in line with Liberal economics. Given his economic freedom by the English Reform Bill, and equivalent legislation in every Northern country, the middle-class man had been allowed to flourish. In counting-house and factory he had been permitted sweated labour, while in the home absolute authority was his. Because these benefits were the fruit of struggle, they could not be yielded up without a struggle even more embittered. Scrooge in England (Solnes in Norway) had fought for the right to vote and for the right to private enterprise in business; his son would have to wait on freedom through a similar period of probation. But the world had changed: the standard of living was increasing; women expected vastly better treatment; medical science had shown how weak lives could be prolonged to dotage. Therefore the period of probation for the son was both more arduous and more lengthy than it had been for the father.

Meanwhile the father wanted some recompense for the years of hardship. And in this he was favoured by the times. Just when a religious sanction would have helped the losing side, if only to redress a human balance, young men and old agreed that religion was at best a personal matter; just when the State should have legislated from the premise that race-suicide was fatal to its continuation and 'becoming', they were both pledged to the Malthusian error—that a race, if small, must of necessity be fine. How ironical it is that the Liberal writers, so provocative, so daring, believed by youth to be saying all the things that youth thought but could not utter—how ironical that they were simply encouraging the old men to have their fling!

VII

When the Liberal Epoch had begun to fade, Strindberg asked one of his many awkward questions: Had they brought up their problems for discussion, only to confess themselves unknowing? Strindberg, rather than Ibsen or Bjórnson, brought this matter to a head; perhaps because he had always been the greatest pessimist among them, perhaps because his own life was so embittered. None of the progressive writers would essay an answer. But even then there were young craftsmen growing up, who would do it soon enough—from their different points of vantage. Selma Lagerlöf would hold that they had failed through ignorance of folk and lore; Knut Hamsun would complain that they had worked to please an urban population; Sigrid Undset would declare that of course they were unknowing: had they not been professedly agnostic?

The various ages of mankind always judge each other harshly, and it may well be that the Scandinavian writers of a later day owed a debt, to Bjórnson especially, which ought to have been paid. To some extent, the children were enjoying a benefit, won by the trial and error of their parents, and a literature was flowering because the ground had been made ready to receive it. But the young writers would not acknowledge any debt whatever. On the whole, theirs was a not unreasonable indictment. They said that Scandinavia had been misrepresented, not only to the world, but also to itself. In their view the North of Europe had possessed always a deep religious faith; it appeared to be socially unconscious only because it had enjoyed a social order, at once equitable and rural, free and ecclesiastically-directed, in days when the South was rent by conflicts; it was feminist beneath an outer crust of man-made legislation, since its women and children were naturally protected and revered.

The indictment was drawn up by people who were wise after the event. They knew that easier divorce did not promote marital felicity, because they had met children whose lives were shattered in the quest for sexual satisfaction; they saw emancipated women who were not contented, urbanized nations which had lost their health, and at least one pacific nation (Belgium, from all sides guaranteed) which had been ravaged by its neighbour. Again, no distinction was allowed between Liberal philosophy in theory and Liberal politics in action. This is not surprising, since the young writers were rebelling against a century which had fashioned thinker and practitioner alike. Mill and Brandes did not teach that the person must be sacrificed to the community of which he was a member. But because they, who were hailed as pioneers of freedom, had not warned their generation how often, when practical problems must be faced, this ideal conception became a mere licence to exploit, many spoke in their name to all the parliaments of Europe. By sins of calculated silence they inspired those demagogues who waged war on Christian education, building their society, not on the natural unit of husband-wife-children, but on a theoretical foundation called the 'State'. Their economic outlook did not see beyond the need for liberty in business; freedom for the strong to sweat the weak; freedom to 'corner' such a necessity as wheat for personal profit; freedom to hold a special 'business' morality without reference to the Ten Commandments. And their liberty of conscience, more spurious than all their other freedoms, was leading from the rejection of Christian Europe to that Nationalism which became in turn the Prussianism of one war and the National Socialism of another.

It is hard to say whether or not Christianity could have made its peace with such a movement. The highest authority is probably Mr. E. I. Watkin, who has written:

> . . . the few Catholics who wished to come to terms with the Liberal State, men such as Lammenais, Lacordaire and Rosmini, failed to perceive that continental Liberalism would make no terms with the Church except those offered by the wolf to the lamb. Its leaders were determined to destroy her influence over the European peoples. . . . Such thinkers as Newman saw that a

merely negative attitude to modern secular thought was not enough
and that sympathetic criticism must disengage from it the truth it
contained. For this he was held suspect. And in fairness it must
be said that the task whose necessity he saw could not at that time
have been successfully accomplished. Only experience and the
advance of thought could show what in modern speculation and
practice is true and valuable. . . . The ideal could not in fact be
realized until the horizontal and immanentist movement had been
developed to the utmost, had unfolded its possibilities, been made
aware of its inherent limitations and provided the material of a
more comprehensive and more organic synthesis.[1]

To this it should be added that the possibilities of secular
philosophy were not made fully manifest until two world-wars
had developed technics beyond the wildest dreams of the
Victorian Liberals, and that it has taken those same wars to
make plain its limitations. Jonas Lie, for instance, however
much he doubted social teaching to be a function of the arts,
leaves little doubt as to the origin of his religious feeling. It
came direct from the young psychologists, whose theories
were then just percolating through the Hapsburg and Hohen-
zollern empires:

Penitence [he wrote, in his introduction to a collection of short
stories] is mankind's first step in his desire to separate himself and
lift himself above the elemental powers, and is followed by all
kinds of magic and mediatory means to force the elemental powers
down. . . . The fear of existence, the great unknown about us,
which is also the foundation of our religious feeling, constantly
shifts its form and name according to the various levels of enlightenment. It lives in the mystical experimentalist at table-turning,
spirit-rapping, and such; in the learned under high-sounding conditions such as the Fourth Dimension; which in the past has in
a sense been the lumber-closet into which a man puts all that cannot
be explained to himself. . . .

It was a far cry from the last, and the best, of Scandinavian
Liberals to those who would react against them.

[1] E. I. Watkin: *Catholic Art and Culture* (Burns, Oates).

VIII

It is untrue to say that progress from one order to another comes about in the heat of battle. What actually takes place is a quickening of senses and perceptions under fire, so that when the storm has died humanity will turn its liberated strength to works of renovation. During the conflict between secular and religious craftsmen in the North of Europe, there was no change in the Christian technique. The orthodox writers conformed, in all essentials, to known and previously accepted patterns. Selma Lagerlöf wanted a return to Evangelical society; and however improbable it was that this would come about, she created a nostalgia for its qualities of class division and co-operation, trust in the printed Word of God, and patriarchal duty. Sigrid Undset's Catholicism was no less clearly dated, for the Church whose triumph she desired was what it had been when Dominic and Francis still lay a little in the future; when the ideal, in architecture, was to build upon a mighty scale, even though the spaces were left empty; in mathematics, movement; in spirituality, the perpetual sacrifice of Mass; in human love, an everlasting search for unattainable perfection. Kierkegaard, despite lavish criticism of all the constituted powers, had nothing new to offer: he held that ghostly knowledge was, if anything, advanced beyond man's ability to use it.

Indeed, the prophecy of Christian forms to come has not as yet been uttered by the Scandinavian writers, but rather by an architect and a musical composer. We shall discuss Sibelius in the proper place, and here we can merely note in passing that the Finnish architect, Lars Sonck, has built at least one church—Berghallis Kyrka at Helsinki—which has no resemblance whatever to former Christian styles. The interesting point is that the first hint of an approaching spring should have come from northern Europe; and our concern must be to welcome its appearance rather than to analyse its message.

Already we can guess that the Third Kingdom—of the

Holy Spirit—foretold by Joachim of Floris in the eleventh century, must sooner or later come to realization. Hitherto the Gospel miracles, although seen as promises and types, have been claimed in themselves as an adequate operation of the Holy Spirit. Thus Christians have possessed light sufficient for one room, yeast for one loaf, and salt for scattered banquets. What can only be described as lack of spiritual ambition spread from the medieval Church to the national sects, and back again to the post-Tridentine Catholic body. ·The Counter-Reformation (an unhappy title !) spoke the language of personal heroics, high policy, and Court intrigue: its vision was not directed to a Christian society; only to a pagan world in which there might be room for Christians. To-day, for the first time since Joachim of Floris made his meditations, the European 'waste-lands' are ·considering the possibility of returning to a universal faith.

It is clear that men cannot evolve from one spiritual ethos to another without some change, in personal feeling, and in outward manners also. Liturgical movements among certain Protestants, and a new interest in the subject on the part of Catholics, are so far symbolic of a desire for unity alone. Should this be all, they will have accomplished very little. A drawing together in face of persecution does not presuppose more light, more yeast, more salt. Yet it is one of many signs that the Third Kingdom is approaching. If old forms suffice no longer, and ancient quarrels lose their meaning, so, too, all hearts are heavy with desire. In short, we learn from literature, architecture, music that the human race, whether alive or dead to the fact that it is doing so, is yearning passionately for God.

Therefore, when the time ·arrives to analyse the literary works of Scandinavian Christians, and when we are struck by their essentially narrow and historic outlook, it must be remembered that they were preparing a good tilth for the one seed whose possibilities are endless. On a prosperous holding one man may plough, one roll, one harrow, and another drive the drill; but each and all are nourished by the harvest.

IX

Apart from their disagreement on the supernatural plane, and thus their polaric advance to meet all other human issues, modern writers of the North have at least a racial tie between them. This, though obvious enough to anyone with a knowledge of the literature of different races, cannot be easy to define. What, in these few excerpts, is specially Irish, English, Scottish ? The quality is there; to analyse might well be to lose it.

First, a snatch of Irish dialogue:

"I don't think I want to go to Heaven," said a rather small girl to me in confession not so long ago.

"And why not ?" I asked.

"Oh," she said, "I wouldn't like to wear a long white robe and a crown and sing hymns all the time."

"What would you like to do ?" I queried.

"I'd like to dance," she said.

"That's fine," said I. "I'm sure you'll get all the dancing you want. And will you please save one dance for me ?"[1]

Secondly, a descriptive passage from an English novel:

In the calm, brown kitchen, alive with the ticking of the grand-father clock . . . the three old folk, like wintered birds, sat round the board in a kind of unconscious thankfulness for mere life and absence of pain. Eli always had the robin cup, the robin being the only bird that did not rouse him to hoarse grumblings about pests and vermin. In the dim past his mother had cajoled and threatened him into a belief that the robin was a sacred bird; so sacred it was. A robin might perch on his spade while he stooped to shake potatoes from the haulm, and he only gave it a crooked smile. Any other bird he would have stoned. They drank from the cups, where the gold was worn at the rim, with a kind of economy of pleasure, as if they felt that the cup of life was slowly emptying, the gold upon it growing faint.[2]

Thirdly, once more the subject of a poor family's repast— this time treated by a Scot:

[1] *Reading in the Refectory*, by Peter Wiffin.
[2] *The Golden Arrow*, by Mary Webb.

"Sit in," she said. Lifting the pan from the crock, she poured the gravy on to the plates. "If it's not tender," she added, "I can do no more with it. Ask the blessing, John."

Her husband lifted his left hand to his brow, which he smoothed for a moment. Then he pronounced the grace that was in the Shorter Catechism. There was a living note of intercession, and his open hand kept moving over his forehead and he closed his eyes. [His wife] could get up and lift a boiling kettle from the fire while her husband was saying grace without destroying the moment's harmony, as if wisdom dwelt also in her movements. . . . The smell of food had been exciting from the beginning. It was rich and good and full of promise. It made hunger merry. It made craving a joy. The rare memory of it would come into lean weeks for long after. . . .[1]

Before endeavouring to see why these passages breathe such a different spirit from each other that they might be translations of three entirely separate tongues, we will consider the overwhelming similarity between modern Northern writers, themselves sundered by everything but race, when they are working on a common theme. The theme is old age, and in each case the character is an ancient landsman.

First, from *God's Peace*—one of Selma Lagerlöf's short stories:

The whole mishap probably arose from the fact that Ingmar Ingmarson had grown old. In his young days a snowstorm would not have made him dizzy. But now everything went round him, as though he had been dancing a Christmas reel. And when he tried to go home he missed the way altogether. He went straight into the great fir wood behind the foddering ground instead of going down to the fields. . . .

He began to be weary of dragging himself through the snow, and several times sat down on a stone to rest. But as soon as he sat down he began to feel sleepy, and he knew that he would freeze to death if he slept. Therefore he tried to keep on moving as the only means of preserving his life. But in spite of all his efforts he could not resist the desire to sit down. It seemed to him that if

[1] *Morning Tide*, by Neil M. Gunn.

he could only rest he did not care much if it should cost his life. He found such a relief in sitting still that the thought of death did not trouble him at all. . . .

Then the thought suddenly passed through him like a shock that it would not be glorious for him to be found frozen to death in the wild wood. He would not like that to be recorded in his obituary. So he rose up again and began to walk on. He had sat still so long that whole masses of snow rolled down from his sheepskin coat when he began to move.

But after a while he sat down again and dreamt. The thought of death became still more welcome to him. He imagined to himself all the details of the funeral and all the respect which would be paid to his dead body. He saw the great table laid for guests in the principal room in the upper storey, the dean and his wife in the seats of honour, the judge sitting there with his white frills spread out over his narrow chest, the major's wife displaying her black silk and thick gold chain wound several times round her neck.

He saw the whole room hung with white—white curtains before the windows, white covers on the furniture. Fir twigs would be strewn along the whole way from the vestibule of the house to the church. . . .

All the village community would be busy providing carriages, all the Sunday hats would be brushed, all the autumn brandy drunk at the funeral feast, all the roads filled with people as though it were a fair-day.

Again the old man started up. He had heard them talking about him as they sat at the funeral feast. "How could he go and let himself be frozen to death in that way?" asked the judge. "What was he doing up there in the great wood?"

The captain answered that he must have been well primed with Christmas ale and brandy.

This roused the old man afresh. The Ingmarsons were sober people. . . .

Next, from *Growth of the Soil*, by Hamsun:

Well, then, here was this stone. Nothing so big to look at above ground, but not to be moved at a touch for all that; it must be a heavy fellow. Isak dug round about it, and tried his crowbar, but it would not move. He dug again and tried once more, but no. Back to the house for a spade then, and clear the earth away, then digging again, trying again—no. A mighty heavy beast to shift, thought Isak patiently enough. He dug away now for a steady while, but the stone seemed reaching ever deeper and deeper down, there was no getting a purchase on it. A nuisance it would be if he had to blast it, after all. The boring would make a noise, and call up everyone on the place. He dug. Off again to fetch a levering pole and tried that—no. He dug again. Isak was beginning to be annoyed with this stone; he frowned, and looked at the thing, as if he had just come along to make a general inspection of the stones in the neighbourhood, and found this one particularly stupid. He criticized it; ay, it was a round-faced, idiotic stone, no getting hold of it in any way—he was almost inclined to say it was deformed. Blasting? The thing wasn't worth a charge of powder. And was he to give it up, was he to consider the possibility of being beaten by a stone? . . .

But then it is that Inger speaks up, a little timidly, again: seeing, no doubt, what is troubling him: "What if we both hang on to the stick there?" And the thing she calls a stick is the lever, nothing else.

"No!" cried Isak furiously. But after a moment's thought he says: "Well, well, since you're here—though you might as well have gone home. Let's try."

And they get the stone up on edge. Ay, they manage that. And "Puh!" said Isak. . . .

Lastly, Sigrid Undset—from *The Master of Hestviken*:

Morning was far advanced when he awoke. There was singing again—they were blessing the palms, he knew, and then would come the procession round the church. Olav still lay abed—once more he was assailed by bitter regret, that he had left home in the clothes he stood in. When at last he came down in his coarse old every-day clothes and heavy boots, the service was already far advanced; the words rang out from the choir:

"*Passio Domini nostri Jesu Christi secundum Matthaeum.*"

From where he stood he could see the priests who were singing. And to-day was the long lesson, so he could not follow it from memory, but only knew some fragments. Wrapped in his old brown cloak he stood far back by the door, and as the clear and powerful male voice intoned the gospel, rising and falling and rising again, he was carried along past words and names he recognized: *Pascha —tradetur ut crucifigatur—Caiaphas—*beacons which told him where they were now. . . .

Olav waited for the words he knew, the words which were branded upon his heart with red-hot irons—would they not come soon? They were not so far away. Ah, now they were coming— now He was sending the Disciples into the city to make ready the supper. Now——

His heart beat against his chest as though it would burst, as the great, rich voice pealed from the choir:

"*Amen dico vobis, quia unus vestrum me traditurus est——*" . . .

"*Numquid ego sum, Domine?*"

Olav felt the sweat break out over his whole body, as the voice of Christ rang out. And then they came, the words that were burnt into his heart:

"*Va autem homini illi, per quem Filius hominis tradetur. Bonum ei si natus non fuisset homo ille.*" . . .

—and the loud voice of Judas followed: "*Numquid ego, sum, Rabbi?*"

The voice of Christ replied: "*Tu dixisti.*"

Olav had bowed his head upon his breast and thrown the flap of his cloak over his shoulder, hiding half his face. The coarse homespun smelt of stable and boat and fish. Among the crowd in festival attire he alone was unprepared. . . .

X

Of all the qualities in race, the quality of humour is the most mysterious. It governs our liking, and probably our detestation also, of a foreign people; and our failure to respond at the moment when others are responding may keep books from us, so that they are in very truth 'sealed books'.

It is diversity of humour which separated the Irish excerpt from the English, and the Scottish from them both. Again, it is a common humour which forged a link between the various Scandinavians. One should not probe too far. . . .

But what Englishman or Frenchman, German or Norwegian could have shown exactly the same degree of understanding, of enveloping though quite impartial sympathy, for a harassed priest and a child at the age of First Communion? In any other literature on earth, one would have been allowed to score. Here the laughter —sweet, uncynical and warm—is directed at humanity in general, as though the writer said: "Our idea of Heaven must seem very curious to the Saints. Young or old—not one of us has seen the Beatific Vision. The confessor and his little penitent both possessed goodwill; and so may God reward them. . . ."

Faith was never questioned, and the source of laughter was our human failure to interpret it correctly. A different quality is found in English writing, even when it flows from the pen of a believer. With whatever small degree of malice, Mary Webb cannot help laughing *at* her people. Eli, having been made to look upon the robin as a 'sacred bird', is a rustic shown off to his superiors. No doubt we all have 'sacred birds', so that the wisest man appears ridiculous through the eyes of the olympian up above him. Class-consciousness and deep-rooted doubt are present here, as they are in every English novel. When jokes are made, they must be made at somebody's expense.

The pith within the crusted Scottish mood is altogether more difficult to fathom. Yet in *Morning Tide* the humour is direct, as it could never be in Irish or in English writing. There are no insinuations, double meanings, facts behind the people which we should guess, though they have not been told us. The smell of food is "rich and good and full of promise" . . . "the rare memory of it would come into lean weeks for long after. . . ." And why should it not do so? The characters are hardworking, thrifty folk, who deserve their simple pleasures. Without analysing, we are intended to respond. Let hunger be merry! Let craving be a joy! Times have been hard enough; and it is right to be uproarious when, in the privacy of his patriarchal kitchen, man strikes a warming moment. . . .

Naturally enough, it is the Scottish mood which brings us closest to the Scandinavian, since the artistic expression of both races is in a major key. Although this renascent work lapses into overtone on very rare occasions, the tones are full and clear and sharp. Having a message to deliver, each craftsman is careful none the less to fill in every detail; and it is such a concern for the minute which provides a similarity of texture between books so different as *Growth of the Soil* and *The Master of Hestviken*. In the first we know the exact thoughts which passed through Isak's head when he was prising up the stubborn boulder: in the second, aware that Olav is about to confess the hidden sin of murder, we share the deep perturbation of an ageing man who has come to church in coarse homespun, smelling of stable, boat, and fish. To examine farther would be to anticipate what follows. If an extra word be needed, let it be the one held dear by Christian scholars through the ages: *Magna est veritas, et praevalebit.* Truth is all that matters.

THE CATHOLIC

SIGRID UNDSET—MEDIEVAL

SOME people come to man through God: others come to God through man. When the second of these movements is a successful journey, and not merely an approach, we praise the happy task which Humanism has accomplished. It seems self-evident that the Humanist saw Divinity in the looking-glass, however cracked and spotted, of his fellow creatures. Very often this is precisely what takes place. Yet it does not do so always. There are certain spirits, and Sigrid Undset's is amongst them, which cannot construe the world in terms less difficult and serious than a free choice for men to win Heaven or reject it. Because they grasp that such freedom is unstinted, they are aware equally of vicious and virtuous occasions. Humanity is not to them a mere battleground where good and evil war; but neither is it a host which must be victorious, because it is by nature with the angels.

This woman novelist, whose literary craft even our present judgment is not afraid to rank above the greatest achievement of George Eliot; whose historic sense, before she was middle-aged, had shown Scott to many of us as an unreliable romantic; and who has dared to herald a return to Catholic Christianity in the land of Ibsen, was nurtured on Liberalism, during a Liberal epoch, and in an ultra-Liberal setting. One side of her family was originally yeoman, from the North of Norway; the other was trading and professional, from Kallendburg in Denmark. Both subscribed to a Protestantism belonging to the final phase: compromising, losing ground, adapting.

At birth Sigrid Undset was endowed with an extraordinary power of penetration. Her father, a travelled man and famous antiquarian, brought home all the leading scholars of his day and country. Sigrid imbibed their splendid talk; yet she did so always with a questioning reserve. The word-pictures which

they painted—of history as a ladder, on the penultimate rung
of which they were at present standing; of faith as the arch-
enemy of reason; of science as a panacea for every mortal ill
—were contrasted in her mind with certain haunting shadows.
Even then her social and sexual knowledge was surprising.
Above all, she had seen the fate of children whose homes were
broken up by adulterous connexions. . . .

At that time (from 1870–1900) Scandinavian literature
agreed, either with the Rationalists in treating sin as a result
of slender education, or with the Neo-Protestants in refusing
to see that it was there. Ibsen demanded a scientific approach
to modern problems, which would at once stimulate discussion
and solve every social question. With this Sigrid Undset was
in full agreement; only, she stated the problems in a very novel
form, and supplied very unexpected answers. Her early
writing, concerned with the humdrum lives of business-girls
in Oslo, was accepted as an inevitable reaction against the
Liberal epoch. These novels taught the sanctity of marriage,
they supplied the Christian answer to Freudian psychology
and commercial ethics, and they suggested that the family
was the most important unit in society. Their message was
moral; it was not new; the Liberals thought that they could
kill it with contempt. Such complacency was to be short-lived.

Because her father had given her an unusual grasp of history,
and because she felt that a student of the Christian tradition
must go back to a time when that tradition flourished, Sigrid
Undset's greatest works were cast in a medieval setting.
Kristin Lavransdatter and *The Master of Hestviken* show
erudition, literary skill, and knowledge of human nature at
their highest peaks separately, and in a partnership whose
profound harmony has not anywhere been rivalled.

They are written gradually, laboriously, and with a patience
which soaks into the spirits of their readers. They neither
excite nor entertain: they win our attention inch by inch;
appealing, not to our sense of the sublime, but to our knowledge
of the normal. Detail is added to detail, circumstance to
circumstance, habit to habit. In the end their characters are

living people. We know them. They are our relations, our
enemies, our friends. No modern novelist has reached a like
perfection in the art of photography through fiction. A man
might spend his whole life in the English countryside and never
meet one of Hardy's rustic chorus; or in a small shop without
a glimpse of Mr. Polly; or with the girls of Mayfair and still
believe that Fleur Forsyte was a myth. Kristin and Olav[1] are
not types: they are battlegrounds on which a supernatural
conflict has to be fought out.

Never before had a novelist approached the Middle Ages
with any but preconceived ideas. Either, as a youth is prone
to ridicule his childhood, they had described a nursery-culture,
abandoned recently for more civilized surroundings; or else,
as Scott did, they had preserved some of the young associations,
rejecting others sternly. Sigrid Undset—and therein lay her
power of provocation—refused to admit that 'civilization' and
'advance' were two terms with but a single meaning. Going
to the Middle Ages with an open mind, she noted the fact
that cultures grow and bloom and fade; that the medieval
arts, and the Catholic religion which inspired them, marked
the fullest blooming of the West; that each falling away from
this ideal was one step more in the retreat from glory.

The Master of Hestviken is a successful adventure of the
imagination, since it deals with the twelfth century, from which
few hard-and-fast records have been handed down; but
Kristin Lavransdatter is a faithful document of life in the
established Middle Ages. The darkened generations which
saw the decline of the Roman Empire and the rise of Benedict-
ine monasticism amidst seemingly endless tribal wars of
Europe had passed from memory to myth. By this time men
knew themselves as Christians, as dwellers in kingdoms under
the pastoral staff of Peter, as vassals under the rulers of those
kingdoms, as fathers of families, and as children of the Church.
They acknowledged three laws, each with its separate sanction:
Canon Law, the law of the land, and the strong local custom
of the district. Against this ordered background conflicts are

[1] Olav Audunsson: chief character in *The Master of Hestviken.*

traced to their sources and followed to their endings. On the one side there is Kristin's devotion to her spiritual, socially-conscious, intensely moral father: on the other the undying passion which she feels for Erlend; a reckless, domineering, yet not wholly unattractive scapegrace. Because each emotion, in its own way, is so exclusive, and felt with so much violence, neither manages to conquer. Finally Kristin turns to God: God whose pale reflection she saw in father and in lover, but to whose real likeness they, limited by many human failings, were not able to attain.

Yet the characters of these two men, and Kristin's love for them, are portrayed in striking contrast from their first appearance until their final passing. While Lavrans dies in bed, fortified by penance, Holy Communion, and the last anointing, Erlend is killed in a brawl. Nor will he receive the Viaticum from their house priest, Sira Solmund. Solmund has slighted Kristin's honour. True children of the Middle Ages, both husband and wife know what such a renunciation must imply, although each places a different emphasis upon it; Kristin accepts the Church's law quite fully: Erlend thinks back to a time when chivalry was all-important, and he is still impatient of a taming gospel.

"Erlend," said she, weeping. "God have mercy on us . . . we must fetch a priest now to you. . . ."

"Ay," said Erlend weakly. "Someone must ride up to Dovre, and fetch Sira Guttorm, my parish priest."

"Erlend—he will not come in time," she said, in dismay.

"Yes," said Erlend vehemently, "if so be God will be gracious to me—for the last office I will not take from this priest that spread lying tales of you. . . ."

"Erlend—for Jesus' sake—you must not talk so . . . let me fetch Sira Solmund to you. God is God, whatever priest may bear Him to us."

"No." The man sat up in bed, so that the coverings slid down from his naked, yellow body. The bandages over his breast and belly were stained anew in bright red patches by the fresh blood that welled forth. "A sinful man I am—God in His goodness grant

me what forgiveness He will: but I feel . . ." He slid back on
the pillows—whispered so that he could scarce be heard. "Not
long enough shall I live to grow so old, and so meek, that I can
suffer—stay quiet in a room with him who lied of you."

"Erlend, Erlend, think of your soul!"

The man shook his head as he lay on the pillows. His eyelids
had drooped close again.

"Erlend!" She clasped her hands; she cried aloud in utmost
need. "Erlend, see you not that, as you have borne towards me,
this *must* needs be said?"

Erlend opened his great eyes. His lips were leaden—but a shadow
of his young smile flitted over the sunken face. "Kiss me, Kristin,"
he whispered. There was somewhat like a shade of laughter in his
voice. "There has been too much else 'twixt you and me, I trow
. . . beside Christendom and wedlock . . . for us easily . . . to
forgive each other . . . as Christian man and wife. . . ."

She called and called his name after him; but he lay with shut
eyes, his face wan as new-cloven wood under his grey hair. A little
blood oozed from the corners of his mouth; she wiped it away,
whispering imploring words to him—when she moved she felt her
clothing clinging cold and wet from the blood she had got upon
her when she led him in and laid him in the bed. Now and then
there was a gurgling sound in Erlend's breast, and he seemed to
draw breath painfully—but he heard no more, and mostlike felt
nothing, as he sank steadily and surely towards the sleep of death.

It would not be true to analyse the contrast between Kristin's
father and her husband by saying that the one was a medieval
and the other a relic from some more simple phase of human
history. Erlend crops up in every age; now as an interior
sickness which casuistry must strive to heal or to allay; now,
externally, as a 'man of the world', or heresiarch, or sceptic.
He is a meeting-place of self-sufficiency with pride in humanity.
He rebels against the Church, not just because he himself knows
better, but because he feels that there should be a different
set of laws for men whose blood runs wild and turbulent within
them. Lavrans was a good Catholic in medieval Norway;
and he would be no less the type, no less excellent of the type,
in twentieth-century Detroit. When she is with him, Kristin

adjusts her love—to embrace his scruples, his seeming hardness, and his occasional harshness. Now he is mortally ill, and they approach a parting:

Some hours later, when Lavrans rode off, his daughter went with him some of the way, walking by his horse's side. . . . It was grievous to look on her despairing face, all marred by weeping. So had she sat in the guest-shed too, all the time, while he ate and talked to the children, jested with them, and took them in his lap, one by one.

Lavrans said softly: "Grieve no more for what you have to repent towards *me*, Kristin. But remember it, when your children grow big, and you may deem that they bear them not towards you or towards their father as you might think was right. And remember then, too, what I said to you of my youth. Faithful is your love to them; I know it well; but you are hardest where you love most, and I have marked that in these boys of yours dwells self-will enow," he said with a little smile.

At last Lavrans bade her turn and go back: "I would not have you go alone any farther from the houses."

They were come into a hollow between little hills with birch trees round their foot and stone screes higher up their sides.

Kristin pressed herself against her father's foot in its stirrup. She groped with her fingers over his clothes and his hand and the saddle and the horse's neck and quarters, rocked her head from side to side, and wept with such a deep lamentable sobbing that her father thought his heart must break to see her plunged in such great sorrow.

He sprang from his horse and took his daughter in his arms, holding her in his embrace for the last time. Again and again he made the sign of the cross over her and commended her to the keeping of God and the holy saints. At last he said that now she must let him go. . . .

Sigrid Undset may have come to Catholicism through a study of the Middle Ages: it is certain that she could not have interpreted the medieval mood had she not first experienced a desire, although perhaps unconscious, to be reconciled with the Catholic Church. Her distrust and ultimate loathing of philosophical liberalism, more especially as it was made manifest in Scandinavia, belongs to an examination of her modern novels—books which deal outright with social questions. Here it is as well to understand that she was in full rebellion against one form of heterodoxy before it had occurred to her that she was a champion of orthodoxy. Yet these in themselves are dangerous terms. Compare Ibsen with St. Thomas Aquinas, and Ibsen is a fool: compare him with Rosenberg or Lenin and he is a phosphorescent ! Folly lies hidden beneath the garments of the wise; successfully because it is as yet no larger than a microbe. Sigrid Undset's reconciliation began from the moment when she saw that the respectable opinion, with its imperceptible power to wreak almighty havoc, would arrive soon enough in cap and bells. She did not pass judgment on things as they were, but on things as they were certain to become.

Writing *Kristin Lavransdatter* and *The Master of Hestviken*, she discovered a truth, which was to be a truism twenty-five years later—that men can exchange the law of God for nothing less than slavery. Over the heads of contemporary Rationalists, she could see gathering shades, where the modern 'Leader' was already lurking. He would find society, not only sated with freedom and turning hard against it, but also—such is the complex coinage of sin—prepared for any counterfeit which had the seeming, however much it lacked the reality, of Divine appointment. Indeed, the Rationalists would emancipate society; as a wilful child might be 'emancipated' from the order of its household, or a bad farmer from the laws of cyclic cultivation. Such cases, carried to their logical conclusions, are bound to end in thraldom.

Sigrid Undset was equally aware that the discipline of faith is a liberating agent. Although medieval man experienced dread—dread of how bad his own business must look through the eyes of Christ and Mary—he knew times of active joy: times when the stones which he had shaped and the glass which he had painted sang back at him; and there was a confluent harmony between animate and inanimate creation. As she

describes the medieval life of cloisters, free farms, and sub-
stantial houses, this secret of old exhilaration comes into her
keeping.

After their wedding, Erlend had taken Kristin home to
Husaby, his manor:

It was the greatest room she had ever seen in any man's dwelling-
house. There was a hearth-place in the middle of the floor, and
it was so long there were two fires on it, one at each end; and the
room was so broad that the cross-beams were borne up on carven
pillars—it seemed to her more like the body of a church or a king's
hall than a room in a manor house. Up by the eastern gable-end,
where the high seat stood in the middle of the wall-bench, closed
box beds were built in between the timber pillars. And what a mass
of lights were burning in the hall—on the tables that groaned with
costly cups and vessels, and on sconces fastened to the walls !
After the fashion of the old age, weapons and shields hung amidst
the stretched-out tapestries. Behind the high seat the wall was
covered with a velvet hanging, and against it a man was even
now fastening up Erlend's gold-mounted sword and his white
shield with the red lion salient.

What delight, too, the people discover in each other—in
the passion from which their children are to be begotten, and
the faith which teaches them that every natural impulse should
be christened !

Erlend took his wife by the hand and led her forward to the
hearth, the guests standing in a half-ring just behind them.

While the married pair stood thus, hand in hand, the priests
were walking the round of the hall, blessing hearth and house and
bed and board.

Next a serving-woman bore forth the keys of the house to
Erlend. He hooked the heavy bunch on Kristin's belt—and looked,
as he did so, as though he had been fain to kiss her where she stood.
A man brought a great horn ringed about with golden rings—Erlend
set it to his lips and drank to her: "Hail and welcome to thy house,
Lady of Husaby !" And the guests shouted and laughed while
she drank with her husband and poured out the rest of the wine on
the hearth-fire. Then the minstrels struck up their music, as Erlend

led his wedded wife to the high seat, and the wedding guests took
their seats at the board.

Because the Scandinavian novel has been used—even more
than the French or Russian novel—as a platform from which
to argue, preach, and make exaggerated claims for many
'systems', there is a risk that its sheer beauty of expression
will become mislaid. Sigrid Undset, for instance, is a writer
of love-stories; a title to fame in America or Britain, and at
least to tolerance in France. Love between the sexes—a mixture
of the lustful, romantic, and ideal—is her continual theme.
Such preoccupation with mankind leaves room, often enough,
for the Fatherhood of God; while it is prone to exclude a
facile worshipping of nature. Those who pay tribute to the
benevolent matriarch—wrought of a soil which is always fertile
and a womb which sheds no blood—calling her 'Mother
Nature', are not the ones who plough or bear or suckle.
With them Sigrid Undset has no sort of kindred. To her the
natural world is beautiful but neutral; a moodless setting and
a disinterested spectator.

When Kristin, together with her little son, is leaving the
farm where she was born, readers live against the landscape
of the Dale. For a short while it becomes their background;
never interfering; never usurping the human faculties of the
memory, the understanding, and the will:

Down behind them lay the Dale, with the river's greenish-white
riband wandering through it, and the farms like small green patches
on the forest-covered slopes. But higher up the upland mosses
arched, brownish or yellow with lichen, inward towards the grey
screes and the bare heights flecked with snowdrifts. Cloud shadows
drifted over the Dale and uplands, but northward all was clear
among the fells; the heaped-up hills had flung off their cloaks of
mist, and shone blue, one behind the other. And Kristin's yearning
moved with the cloud-flecks northward on the long road that lay
before her. . . .

Hardy, opening *The Return of the Native* upon Eglan
Heath, committed himself to neither less nor more. Dale and

heath are quite impersonal. Treading their ground, man may
rob or lust or murder; or else he may love and work and
worship. They do not care; they cannot intervene; they are
in a sleep from which no sound will wake them.

In *The Master of Hestviken* human folly—even the potential
sin of growing children—is contrasted with the reposeful world
around them. Olav and Ingunn, experiencing the first torments
of a mutual passion, are journeying with an old battle-axe
towards the Hamar smithy:

At high-water mark, where beach and greensward met, the path
led by a cairn. The boy and girl stopped, hurried through a Pater-
noster and an Ave, and then each threw a stone upon the cairn as
a sign that they had done their Christian duty by the dead. . . .

They had to cross the stream in order to reach the point where
Olav had thought he could borrow a boat. This was easy enough
for him, who walked barefoot, but Ingunn had not gone many
steps before she began to whimper—the round pebbles slipped
under her feet and the water was so cold that she was spoiling
her best shoes.

The sky was now blue and cloudless, and the fjord quite smooth
with small patches of glittering white sunshine. Its bright surface
reflected the land on the other shore, with tufts of light green foliage
amid the dark pine forest and farms and fields mounting the hillside.
It had become very warm—the sweet breath of the summer day was
heavy about the two young people. . . .

All through life the pebbles would be slipping from under
Ingunn's feet; and it would be Olav's task to shield her, not
only from a personal waywardness, but also from his own
breach of Christian law and order. Such a consequential
view of sin leaves little room for happy endings. What love
there is when passion has been spent becomes a rarefied
emotion; duty has refined it, and habit, and the protection
which strong natures must afford the weak ones. Sigrid
Undset's women are reluctant to yield before the urge of
passion. They may love wilfully and wildly; but they bear a
grudge against their lovers—the awakeners and tempters.

Olav's first thoughts of this girl, whom in boyhood he would betray and from whom, in manhood, he would see the health and zest ooze out like water fallen on parched clay, are not especially romantic:

He never thought whether she was fair or not. Tore was fair, it seemed to him, perhaps because he had heard it said so often. Ingunn was only Ingunn, near at hand and everyday and always at his side: he never thought of how she might be, otherwise than as one thinks of the weather; that has to be taken as it comes. He grew angry and scolded her when she was contrary or troublesome —he had beaten her too, when they were smaller. When she was kind and fair-spoken with him and the other boys, their playmates, he felt happy as in fine weather. And mostly they were good friends, like brother and sister who get on well together—at whiles they might be angry and quarrel, but neither thought the other's nature could be changed from what it was.

Sigrid Undset thinks and compels these people into being, as an old woman might mutter to herself beside the fire— recalling in her ancient loneliness those who in youth were close about her. There is a sad wisdom, borne alike by characters and situations, which gives rise to the question as to whether she was at any time young in mind and spirit. "Neither thought the other's nature could be changed from what it was. . . ." Such a line could only have been written by one who had shared the Church's disappointments. The sentiment is Catholic, but it stresses the sombre half of Catholic experience: Peter's barque has known more tempests than calm weather, while the saint himself is remembering those hours which followed cock-crow. It may not discard totally the chance of swift and permanent conversion, but the room it leaves is for baptismal grace to grow, helped on by penance and Communion, as crops ripen, though not perceptibly, when they are cleaned and nourished.

Had she then no sense of humour? Certainly she lacked a sense of the grotesque. It could not be otherwise in one who valued dignity, seeing the creature always compassed about by his Creator. Yet there are delightfully warm places amidst the gloom and brooding. When Kristin is a little girl, Lavrans rides with her every year to the Midnight Mass at Christmas. She is put in a sack of hay across his saddle, with only her small face exposed to bitter weather. Fearing it may become frozen as they ride along, Lavrans now and then leans forward, biting her nose upon its tip. When she fails to scream, he rubs it with fox-fat, which he carries in his pocket. The light touches are not very obvious; and readers, provoked by a major challenge, are always apt to miss them.

It is surprising that she should have achieved a foremost place, which may be pride of place, in Scandinavian letters. This would have been quite impossible a half-century ago. Then Agnosticism was triumphant; and the religious opposition, as voiced by Kierkegaard in Denmark and Selma Lagerlöf in Sweden, repudiated the medieval Church no less vigorously than it was repudiated by the sixteenth-century Reformers. The truth may be that both sides in Scandinavia had judged Catholicism and the Middle Ages so blindly that their judgments were bound to modify directly passion cooled. Again, by 1920 actual experiments in living had reached a point there which they were not to reach in England until a decade later. Slavery and licence—the logical outcome of a neo-paganism —were examined; men realized that present standards were disastrous, and they approached the old ones calmly. Sigrid Undset had forced a diagnosis: in her modern books she was to recommend a cure.

SIGRID UNDSET—MODERN

ANY study of Sigrid Undset is bound to fall far short of the ideal. Most writers develop naturally from apprenticeship, through proficiency, and upwards to whatever niche is awaiting them in the hierarchy of letters. They are influenced, of course, by events in their home-circles, no less than by happenings in a wider world. Reading their books in the order of production, it should be possible to guess when they fell in love; when they were very poor; when their spirits were cowed by an outbreak of national folly or broken on a wave of international madness. These are ordinary landmarks. We find them in the correspondence of men and women who are not professional writers. Sigrid Undset is elusive because she passed through three phases, which were almost separate lives, and which produced literary harvests, each one unique as barley, wheat, and oats. There was a time before the leap, a time of the leap, and a time of after leaping.

During the first phase she was aware of the social and sexual questions which she would answer in the prime of craftsmanship, as a growing child feels maturity tugging at its senses. Like childish dreams, the earliest books are vague and veiled; for the knowledge of life which they possess comes out in swift, ill-tempered rushes—only to betray an abysmal ignorance of human nature. They are interesting because they are prophetic. The young woman who created *Jenny* must either have committed suicide or become a Christian confessor. She was more of a Puritan then than she would be when drawing obvious morals; Jenny Winge—"of the fair face and kind voice"—is hounded to death by a pagan conscience. Such a conscience tells its victims that earthly happiness is of supreme importance; that to wound the Ego is the sin which cannot be forgiven. This transient composure (not life, not supernatural) is mortgaged by too much self-indulgence; it requires a nice adjustment, and a search towards it fans the fear that a balance is hard to find and impossible to hold. *Jenny* is a pagan book: it was inspired by terror.

This was before the leap. The leap itself was approached by Sigrid Undset much as it had been by Newman and Augustine. They saw—in Neo-Gothic England and Magian Africa respectively—a narrow gateway leading to limitless horizons; and it was the same opening vista which lay ahead of her in Norway. Once through, she was accused, naturally enough, of making propaganda. As the word 'criticism' is used more and more in a wholly adverse sense, so too this 'propaganda' has become associated with lying—or at least with reckless overstatement. There is a danger that the presentation of any case at all, however fair and objective it may be, will remain unheard by those for whom it has not some previous measure of attraction. No habit of mind could militate so much against the truth. Had it set in a hundred years ago, children would still be sweated in the mines, approach to government be thwarted, and debtors be languishing in prison. Sigrid Undset, throughout her modern books, does present the Catholic case; and to a public which might not otherwise have heard it. No Newman lived in Scandinavia to hammer this home in splendid prose; no Francis Thompson to capture its rarer qualities in verse: a whole people awaited the twentieth century and that century's chosen form, the novel.

Were such a presentation the only virtue of her modern books, it could be argued that a Catholic answer had been delivered with more weight, by the Sovereign Pontiffs. Yet official pronouncements need to be restricted, since they move from the general to the personal, rather than from one known case to the universe around it. These books have the solid virtue of presenting whole lives for our inspection; lives which meet religion, as they meet with money, passion, work, romance, and all the other facets of existence. If Sigrid Undset knows how men argue with their parents, whisper to their loved ones, and appeal to the fancy of their children, she is no less sure that they must exclude the home from business, and colleagues of the day from the home-circle of the evening.

Although Kristin, Uni of *Images in a Mirror*, Lucy Arnesen and Julie Selmer of *The Wild Orchid* and *The Burning Bush*, its sequel, are but a few instances of durable feminine characters which she was able to create, her outstanding power is the ability to think, speak, and reason as a man. This she shares with a minute company of woman-writers; perhaps with none save Charlotte Brontë, who worked in a literary age, and Sheila Kaye-Smith, who was cast into one less fertile. She knows that there is—in bad men, in rough and reckless men, in men blinded by their passions or throttled by their pride— a longing to be recognizable as the sons of God. When terrible situations strip them bare of all pretence, she allows them to say this, repeatedly and boldly. For others such a presentation of masculine psychology could very well be dangerous: they would portray 'reformed' characters and downright prigs. Sigrid Undset navigates this Scylla, for she admits that both sexes are tempted with equal violence by the flesh. Yet women are always the more plastic, and men have a deep responsibility towards them. Her noble men—noble because they do strive against a darkness within them to become the sons of light— understand that one of the worst obstacles which they have to overcome is a desire to treat their women as less than fully human. Lavrans, Olav, and still more the modern man, Paul Selmer, know that true womanhood was revealed in Mary; that they have a duty to discover her afresh in daughters, wives, and mothers.

In *The Wild Orchid*, Selmer's conflict is due, partly to normal masculine shortcomings, partly to the peculiar economic circumstances of the modern world. For he is at once old enough to fall in love and too young to shoulder those responsibilities which gather round any moral relationship between the sexes. In a different society—which would have allowed him and Lucy to rear a quantity of children—a mutual attraction and a sharing of trials, anxieties, and reliefs must have welded them together. In the twentieth century their love becomes a problem and a burden. A noble character would sacrifice personal freedom and social standing to bring about a marriage:

Selmer, at that time, was merely average. Therefore the lesson of his early life is that the finest clay alone will survive a modern testing. By the end of the book he has made a marriage with the second-best: in *The Burning Bush* he sees this 'second-best' deteriorate before him—from a petted girl to an immoral woman.

Even then he is putting up a fight. How well he argues!— for instance, with his Evangelical relations, against a verse of Grundvig:

> To bid the world farewell aright
> In life's fair dawn or evening light
> Is hard for one and all;
> We ne'er could learn it here below,
> Did we not feel Thee near and know,
> Jesu, Thou'lt hear our call.

In the first place [says Selmer] it isn't true at all. To bid the world farewell aright—that's exactly what men have always been able to do; whatever they believed or didn't believe, they've always had the courage to die. It's no more than natural that men should insist on courage and pride being stronger than the fear of death— though it isn't everyone that succeeds in taking the last fence handsomely. The young—and the irreligious—often manage it best —any doctor or nurse you like to ask will tell you something about that. It is *living* without religion they don't manage so well, or at any rate they don't succeed in living *well*, and getting on in the world, without becoming odious and vulgar and narrow and egotistical—*that* may be an argument for the truth or anyhow the necessity of religion. But as to any real horror of death—that only comes in when one begins to mix up Jesus in it, and judgment-day, and all that. So I don't give much for all this talk about Christianity being essentially a means of comforting the sick and dying. As a narcotic at any rate it's a complete fiasco.

To the drawing of her priest-characters she brings the same insight, shrewdness, and disciplined reserve as she does to the bolder portraits of men who face sexual and economic facts from close, subjective quarters. While in her medieval books the good clerics are nearly always monks (she likes particularly rough-spoken, hard-shelled Benedictines), her priest of *The Wild Orchid* is a secular, engaged upon the mission. This one-time sportsman, Father Harold Tangen, speaks only when he must, and then with a directness which explains his customary silence. Selmer, anticipating reproaches and an emotional warming-up, takes him the problem of illicit love:

". . . what I'm wondering is, if it goes on the way it seems to be going, getting more and more difficult for young people to marry or to afford to have children before they're well on in years—so that the community gets accustomed to us young people making marriages of conscience or entering into un-Platonic engagements, and is no longer scandalized about it—don't you think the clergy will follow suit and discover that we're not such arrant sinners after all? Since what we're doing is no longer in conflict with civic morality? You see, I remember, when I went to school, it was such a terrible thing to be a freethinker or a child of a freethinker—now even the parsons—or the young ones at any rate—are quite ready to admit that freethinkers may be decent folk. And at that time, too, they thought that divorce was frightfully ungodly. . . ."

"I see," said the priest. "What you want to know is, whether the Catholic Church condemns irregular connexions of the kind you tell me about on an immutable principle?"

"Precisely. No more than a year ago I couldn't see any reason why Lucy and I should give up more than we jolly well had to. Of course we knew it would be many years before we could have a home and a child, but what was the use of imposing unnecessary restrictions on ourselves? But now I at any rate have come to feel that perhaps there may be reasons—which exist independently of whether current morality at a given time may cry shame on corrupted youth, or whether it may treat young people in an easygoing fashion, saying they can't be expected to exercise self-denial until they're old and grey and can afford to marry. . . ."

Now there is a weakness here on which Sigrid Undset does not lay her finger. Perhaps Father Tangen's silence is pregnant with other meaning—if so, it seems to non-Catholics, and to many of the Faithful, a conspiracy of silence, which is shared

by more than Scandinavian clerics. Irregular connexions are
condemned on an 'immutable principle'; but are there not
principles, no less immutable, which condemn the joint-stock
company for paying starvation wages, and the slum landlord
for putting up mean and noisome dwellings? It would be
curious to hold that sexual morality could flourish in an
unrighteous society; for these problems interlink. People
cannot marry unless the man has a fair wage and the woman
a clean home: they cannot have children in a setting which is
loaded against the chances of survival. True it is that the world
must be a 'vale of tears'; true that Popes have denounced
instigators of social evil and those who pander to it: a suspicion
remains that the rank and file of clerics would rather chastise the
poor than irritate the wealthy. This suspicion neither Tangen
nor his creator manage to allay.

Certainly a book yields a different message to each reader
who bothers to give it his attention; and each one finds,
sooner or later, what he is out to seek. Of three people reading
Sigrid Undset's novels, the first might say that she desired
to paint an accurate picture of Norwegian life; the second,
that she was reacting hard in favour of the Middle Ages;
the third, that she was making rather clumsy propaganda.
None of these judgments is more than superficial. Ibsen,
dreading a cosmopolitan verdict against the native culture,
was consciously Norwegian; so also was Knut Hamsun,
when he distrusted the eastward flowing of American ideas—
speed for the sake of speed, and the romance of business.
Sigrid Undset's allegiance is to the whole of Christendom,
and in a secondary sense alone to Scandinavia. Because her
love is reserved for sanctity unblemished—Kristin gives herself
to Erlend out of marriage only to rue it ever after—she may
be called a Medieval; yet she is equally competent to tackle
the most modern of material, since she has no feeling confined
in less than time, and no belief enclosed in less than space.
The charge against her of making propaganda is a good one
—good if we hold that art is an absolute rather than a relative.
But how many to-day hold that it has, or ever had, absolute

existence ? Is it not always, and inevitably, the servant of human fashions, faiths, and causes ?

Indeed, the Catholic prognosis of contemporary disease is stated with relish in the modern novels. Although *The Burning Bush* is not upon the mediocre level of *Ida Elizabeth*, Sigrid Undset's one full-length literary lapse, it contains passages which are bound to jar in foreign translations. Selmer, becoming a very zealous Catholic, is not faced with a half- or quarter-orthodox society, but with one wherein heresy is ubiquitous and active. If the ardour of these Norwegian Catholics seems a little overpowering, their stupendous task has to be considered; so also has the clarified air which Scandinavians breathe: everything they grasp is taken 'by the horns'. The challenge of this book is found when we contrast Selmer's regenerated character with those, still unregenerate, around him. His wife lacks charity, even for herself, because she has no faith: Lucy, his boyhood love, is bereft of hope. She *knows* that the worst is bound to happen, looking upon as simply callow those happier mortals who strive to reassure her.

Sigrid Undset's women, however, are always less convincing then her men. Randi Alme, a young girl in *The Wild Orchid* and a teaching-nun in *The Burning Bush*, is made to hold forth at astonishing length on most unlikely themes. When Selmer, enjoying a second honeymoon, runs across her in a Parisian café, she begins a breathless monologue at once:

O God—there was a little girl here once. She wanted to be an operatic singer. Slightly deformed—she had evidently suffered frightfully from rickets as a child—and then she had a face like a camel, and her arms were much too long. There was no beauty in her voice either, but it was extremely powerful. And this unfortunate child, you see, lest life should pass her by, as she said—and somebody had put it into her head that she must have an affair before she could really become an artist. She was ready to go to any depth of humiliation—and—depravity in order to find one. You understand, ugly as sin and a nymphomaniac—that was the impression she gave me in any case. Enough to make one weep.

Then there are all those who are born with some kind of repression
—so that their very inclinations run in an opposite direction to the
ordinary—unnatural, as it is called, though often enough it is
their nature. . . .

From an intelligent woman, who had been a long time
under vows, such a formidable speech would not be surprising:
from the lips of a young girl, it taxes our credulity too far.
The more so when she is described as:

. . . really very pretty . . . she had a little triangular face,
the kind of pink and white complexion that goes with red hair and
freckles, and big grey eyes with long reddish-blonde lashes. And
then she was neat—in a blue walking-dress with a pink blouse;
there was something tidy about her from the blue hat with a mass
of violets underneath the brim against the splendid dark red hair,
to the tips of her little brown buckled shoes that peeped out under
her skirt. . . .

The picture is feminine enough: the preoccupation with
abstract moral problems is not feminine at all. Then again,
Sigrid Undset hopes we shall believe that this girl was Selmer's
chance—his chance to embrace the Catholic religion and
domestic serenity in one rewarding armful. Yet, thinking
of him as Randi's husband, we can forget, neither that a
potential nun who marries must spoil more than her vocation,
nor that she judged character too shrewdly. One woman who
describes another as, 'deformed' and 'camel-faced' might
well, after careful taming, be an asset to the order of St. Bridget:
in the home she could not be so soothing!
If this were Selmer's chance, he was in any case fated to
mislay it. No direct or obvious happiness on earth is in keeping with Sigrid Undset's view. To her the world is a place of
heavy travail; two classes of good deed are open to the pilgrim:
a rapid pressing forward and a constant sharing of his neighbour's burden. Human nature, at its best, is wavering and
fragile: possessing the good, men hanker for the evil; and if
at last they do arrive in Heaven, this is attributable more to

the strong charity of God than to their own uncertain efforts.

Only when she contemplates the love of a God Who was born in vagrancy and done to death in shame, does she become less tragic and more tranquil. What a tangible calm there is in her meditations on *Christmas and Twelfth Night* !

It is so beautiful out of doors this evening; I go down into the garden to say my Rosary. It is autumn and the evening is dark, but the sky is full of stars: a great big one hangs low in the south-east, behind the weeping birches—they are beginning to get thin in the leaf now; their crowns stand out so clearly, delicately etched against the dark blue, star-strewn heaven. . . .

It is Friday night, so it must be the Sorrowful chaplet. Alas, its mysteries seem incredibly far away to-night. There was once another garden, bathed in the blindingly white moonlight of sin which makes all shadows black as ink. In the very blackest darkness lies a man on his face praying, and his sweat falls like drops of blood on the earth. And the man is both God and man. The immeasurable space around him is filled with hovering suns and spheres—his stars which he has placed in the eternal ring-dance of the worlds. And on this tiny earth on which he has chosen to sojourn his moon shines clearly over waste oceans and over waving treetops, wild and sturdy forests where no person has yet pushed his way to spoil them with the ferocity and paltriness of humanity. All is his. And this little sphere alone is full of unutterably beautiful things. . . .

Even here she cannot contemplate the Holy Family for long without dwelling upon sins against the home and marriage. With deadly effect she quotes these exclamations from the brutal prose of Louis Veuillot[1]:

, "Dr. Lebon, Dr. Lebon, you are a learned man, you know that mankind is endowed with a kind of taste for child murder ! This phenomenon is to be found in all latitudes, in all civilizations, and among all barbarians. It is tolerated on one ground or another: to guard the nation's strength, to honour the gods, to fête the spirits, to get outside the law of the firstborn, to spare expense and the

[1] Author of *Les Odeurs de Paris*.

trouble of education; in Athens, Sparta, Carthage, Rome, Pekin, Tahiti, London, Paris and its surroundings—children are murdered, or men sorrow that they have been born. It is only Christianity that has the power to combat this extraordinary habit, and where Christianity fails that which has been conquered resumes its bloody sway. . . ."

Although she cannot bring herself to hate the town—her descriptions of Trondhjem and Oslo in the modern books do not compare unfavourably with those of Husaby and Hestvik in the medieval Sagas—she knows that the restless chase of wealth and pleasure, always predominant when technical achievement is most rapid, must victimize little children and old or helpless people. While her senses respond to the sight of splendid buildings and to the sound of quick feet on city pavements, her Christian conscience is aware that houses hold grim secrets; that abortionist and pervert move in the throng of innocent, light-hearted people. When her characters fall in love with some corner of a city, they need to justify their joy, in the face of moral precepts.

As she grew accustomed to the faith of her adoption, this conscience did not gnaw so fiercely; even as Catholic propaganda, *Images in a Mirror* is more telling than the long-drawn life of Selmer. That discussed, not only faith and works, religious authority, celibacy, ritual, but also the freeing of men's intellects by the Liberal writers and the liberation of Norway from Swedish dominance, which took place during the action of the novels. The canvas was too large and the details too confusing. *Images in a Mirror* is a welcome contrast. Here delicate relationships—between husband, wife, and children; between an ageing woman and a lonely man who desired to be her lover; between comparative prosperity and squalor—are woven upon a strong, resilient framework. The Church is never mentioned. Instead, all that she has to say to modern men; of fidelity to precepts of perfection; of courage in poverty, and of poverty itself as a thorn which can be made to blossom, is breathed in a silence of suffering and meditation. Sigrid Undset had understood that she must not speak for a minority alone. A cosmic thinker still, she had been given criteria for the testing of all problems, and roots which could feed continually upon the stored-up wisdom of the ages. In this book she is not justifying the faith: she is living the life, and living it more fully.

On the final page, her whole outlook on the world—on the world with its joyful and sorrowful mysteries, and its glorious mysteries also—is condensed into the most homely of all settings. As Nora slammed the door on her home and husband, Uni has come back again to hers. So perhaps must the urbanized, unfertile woman receive an answer, in living and in action, from the instinctive mother:

And she got up with Lasse in her arms, carried him over to his cot, and covered him up. She turned the baby over and picked up his quilt, which he had kicked on to the floor, laid it over him, and tucked it well in.

THE PROTESTANTS

SÓREN KIERKEGAARD

To understand why we can never hope to understand this theologian, philosopher, devil's advocate at the court of King Demos, and eternal plaintiff in the court of love, it is necessary first to illuminate with a hard light, and even with a searchlight, the years in which he worked. They are known as the 'Hungry Forties': they are more aptly described as the 'Roaring Forties'. Their electric tempests broke, not between America and Europe, but upon both continents; and everywhere with equal violence. They were the more terrible because they took their time: now threatening, and now approaching nearer; now promising the poor man that he would sweat no longer; now causing the rich man to break out in a sweat of horror. They boded a revolution, which would rise assuredly to the bloodstained height of civil conflict; reprisals by some nation which was being starved to death, or by some class whose daily round was at best a living torment. The world might lose trade and money: it had lost faith in God.

Wealth, as never before in Gothic culture, was worshipped as a thing in itself; as a legitimate sole object of pursuit. The human brain was dazzled, and the human senses charmed —by their own achievements. Prosperity, hope in the future, contentment with the present, all rested underground, on coal. Coal was driving the 'tin kettle' across the Atlantic and round the Cape to India; providing dividends for gentlemen 'of independent means' and for countless maiden ladies; speeding the brutalized convicts and the starving Irish to Australia; sucking down small children to labour in darkness for their betters. It was not a safe foundation on which to build a house —it divided up the household. In a landed society there had been high and low, walking worthily on their different levels.

In an underground society there were some who could not walk at all. . . .

Historians have been slow to recognize that a given time is intelligible only when we know how men of that time approached religious questions. As the new textbooks will devote chapter upon chapter to bombings and mechanized campaigns — with but a hurried footnote on the burning of devotional writings and consecrated buildings — so the old ones harp the brazen tune of revolution and never touch the wistful note of an expiring faith. Outward events, in the eighteen forties, were sufficiently momentous; but they resulted from a stern rejection of Divinity and a passionate prostitution of humanity. To hold it there is to have it in perspective.

1848 was the year of climax. In England the Reform Bill, having shifted power from the Whig oligarchy to the middle classes, left the poor, both urban and rural, to suffer exploitation without representation. The Chartist Rising, when it came, was treated in much the same fashion as was the General Strike of 1926; a combination of operatives in many trades was nothing less than treason. In France, where the way had been prepared for them by the lax government of Louis-Philippe, the Socialists did arrive in office. Their political education was so slender, and their economic theories so inflexible, that they were removed in favour of a military dictatorship—to be followed shortly by the Second Empire. In Germany the situation was more complex. An 'all-German' parliament at Frankfurt, striving to kill the Vienna Settlement, found that the King of Prussia would not join the other princes in a universal abdication. While National Socialism was postponed for ninety years, the *Junkers* facilitated its eventual coming. At this same time the New York papers were reporting that life had never been more gay nor suicides more frequent: Irish peasants hymned 'The Green Fields of America' while, on their own fields, potatoes were turning to black slime. Crops rotted, railways boomed; children starved, old men lived in comfort. Everything was moved by coal; every being and nation rocked unsteadily upon it.

In Denmark two events were taking place: the first, since it concerned a king, was thought to be momentous; the second, affecting only a young writer, was not noised beyond his own immediate circle. Christian VIII was invited to cede some territory to the German *Reich*: when he refused, the Wilhelm-strasse described him as 'provocative' and 'an arch-menace to the peace of Europe'. Meanwhile the young writer, Sóren Kierkegaard, was undergoing conversion. In boyhood, cold and hungry, while pasturing sheep on barren heathland, his father had uttered curses against the Majesty of God. From that moment, as though in proof of His existence, God had permitted him to prosper. The starving shepherd became a successful business man in Copenhagen. But, wherever he went, the sense of guilt went with him. In due time it was loaded on his son. Sóren, passing through a phase of unbelief, when he had lived a-morally and wildly, halted upon the very frontier of damnation. Suddenly the realization dawned —that a father's sin might well be visited upon his children.

Born in 1813, but failing to live by his pen until 1843, he was a late beginner; late for an individual writer; later still for one who would decide the religious future of a country. In other lands religious leaders had long since tried to meet the challenge of a society uprooted from the fields and thrust upon the streets. For twenty years Newman had been endeav-ouring to strengthen the Anglican Communion; to give it authority, and to provide it with some sanction, which could be used against the proud ungodly. Forced to admit himself defeated, he had transferred his allegiance from Canterbury to Rome, and his energies from Oxford to the Midlands. The second orientation was less spectacular, but of no less importance than the first one. At Oxford life was still cultured and secluded: at Birmingham life was in the raw. There, in the mean alleys which petered out on slag-heaps, in sight of furnaces and sound of forges, disease, spiritual and physical, was raging. While at Oxford parsons were advised, somewhat testily, to acquaint themselves with the works of Continental Liberals, Midland labourers implored food and respite for their bodies, and occasionally Manna for their souls. There the religious life of England was rooting in fresh pastures, just as French Catholicism was showing a new vigour in the young towns north and east of Paris.

The spiritual state of Denmark, on the other hand, seemed to be passing painlessly from stagnation to decomposition. Occasional fits of zeal, which in any case troubled only one minister in fifty, or a village without means to communicate its message, were directed inwards; they were used up on self-improvement, rather than radiated outwards. Unlike the systems of Calvin and Ignatius—the two extremes which meet —Lutheranism is not a sociable and still less a revolutionary religion. It favours—though generally as a despairing counsel —the sense of corporate duty; it frowns alike on civic responsibility and social conscience. It makes good soldiers, but very poor civilians; contented sexagenarians, but restless adolescents; pious folk who will turn their emotions inside out on Sundays, but who shudder at the thought of turning the world upside down on weekdays. In the last analysis, they regard every secular endeavour as 'fallen' and past praying for.

This was not a well-stocked armoury, and it was to prove quite useless against those evil forces which had been unleashed by the Industrial Revolution. Farther north, men conserved some of the old devotional habits; they saw a homely significance in the use of bread at the Lord's Supper, and they were still as they had been two centuries before—when they had mistaken Lutheran missionaries for Papal envoys.[1] In Denmark all ties with the cultural past of Europe had been sundered firmly. Small and never self-contained, meeting Prussia across an inland frontier on the south, she felt herself to be at the mercy of Germany's ambitions. Sometimes these might be spiritual or intellectual; they were more often greedy and material. The result, in any case, was a national complexity of outlook. Seeing their own character as 'open, naif, innocent, and true', the Danes wondered whether a race, endowed with such attributes alone, could survive in the midst of a

[1] See *Divided Christendom*, by the Abbé Congar (Geoffrey Bles).

realistic world. At one moment everything German was the fashion; at the next it was ridiculed and hated. From Berlin, they turned instinctively to Paris.

It may well be that *le génie latin* lies in an ability to fuse the most solid and conservative traditions with an apparent disrespect towards the past, and a keen joy in every fleeting fashion. Latin peoples understand how this can be done, and they seldom overdo it. But when Northerners, possessing a very different *génie*, go to Paris for cultural stimulation and rejuvenation, they find a barren cosmopolis rather than a market-town, which makes room for political and philosophical extremists—because they are so rare. Danes of the nineteenth century saw a cradle of anti-religious legislation: they did not dream that it was also the cradle of Monsieur Olier and the Sulpician schooling.

Kierkegaard shared the outlook, together with all its limitations, of his time and people. Although he had travelled, studying and writing at Berlin, he remained no less a Scandinavian than did those talkative, blue-eyed, fair-haired adolescents whom one met in the cafés of the Friedrichstrasse or Boul' Miche between the two world-wars. So very much was never destined to concern him; and it is easier to define his spirit by that which lay beyond its scope than by that which it could mill. Nowhere, for instance, does he dwell upon the Incarnation —that paradox of faith which, above all others, has strengthened the mystic and consoled the weak throughout the Christian ages. Such men have compared the Blessed Trinity with pagan deities, and they have been startled into reverence because, while the gods were cruel and arrogant and eventually sub-human, God Incarnate could afford to stoop from the height of heaven to a manger and a cross. This comparison has led to contemplation; a contemplation which loves to dwell upon the earthly sojourning of God; it sees the Infant Jesus blessing mortal babies; Christ the carpenter working beside His brother-craftsmen; Christ applying the merits of His Passion to the anguished, the outcast, and the dying.

Kierkegaard did not—as the Calvinists had done—reject

these pictures, on the ground that they must lead inevitably
to superstition. Lying outside his brief, it is doubtful whether
he noticed them at all. For he was a man, both of complexity
and concentration; of febrile genius and dogged perseverance;
a Puritan yet a lover of fine clothes, good manners, personal
conviviality and civic pomp. The brief which he took up was
against the Established Church in Denmark, and it was this
institution which he pounded with self-torturing ridicule and
mirthless laughter. What relish he puts into the following
quotation, from a play by Holberg! It is a cynical deacon
(for Kierkegaard, the authentic modern churchman) who is
holding forth:

"Before my time people in the village considered all funeral
hymns equal; but I have carried it so far that I can say to a peasant:
'Which psalm do you want? The one costs so much, the other
so much'; likewise if earth is to be cast on the dead: 'Do you want
fine sand or common clay?'"[1]

Shaw writes, in the preface to *John Bull's Other Island*, that each
Christian communion is bound to land some queer fish into its
nets. Children are baptized, not only according to the religious
traditions of their parents, but also according to the convergence
of latitude and longitude on which they have been born.
The Protestants 'catch' many natural Catholics: the Roman
Church is sometimes baffled by the training of those who are
sceptical by nature. Fish from Eastern waters stray into the
West; there are also archaic and atavistic fish; and fish whose
species has yet to be defined. When Kierkegaard was taken
to the font, the communion of his fathers had been reached a
scorpion.

In nineteenth-century Denmark tentative reforms were
taking place. These were not so much upon the English model
as germs of the *Hochkierche*, a movement which blossomed,
after eighty years, into the writings of Sóderblom in Sweden
and Heiler in Berlin. From first to last this movement was

---

[1] *Fear and Trembling* (Oxford University Press).

seeking to restore objective values in place of subjective or emotional thinking; to teach that the sacraments were medicine for the sick rather than ambrosia for the pious; to make communal worship once more the prototype of common living. Kierkegaard neither trusted the leaders nor did he understand their terms of reference. To him all religious thought was naturally subjective; enriched by the emotions, because they formed a sixth sense, granted expressly for the purpose. His fear lest the sacraments should be fed to dogs led him to set aside the children; and the more they were winnowed by his teaching, the fewer and farther between he discovered them to be. As for public worship: if two or three chose to assemble in the name of God, God would surely hear them. Yet an overriding consideration was the Ego—the stranger in a carnal land who had known, miraculously, the voice of his Creator.

The individualism, encroaching upon the very Gospel, brands him as liberal, ultra-civilized, and Western. It is poles apart from Khomiakov, who could write:

The loneliness of man is the cause of his impotence; whosoever separates himself from the people creates a desert around him. . . .

and from Soloviev, who held that even Russian Orthodoxy would not fulfil its destined mission while it was sundered from other Christian communions.[1] Khomiakov and Soloviev believed no less firmly in a dynamic spiritual society than Marx did in his 'dialectical materialism'. For him the nomad order was bound to change into the feudal, the feudal to the bourgeois, and the bourgeois to the proletarian; for them the Church, here on earth, was bound to grow into perfection—nothing would stay until Christ's Kingdom was established. This is a typically Russian point of view. Kierkegaard came no nearer to an understanding of it than a German composer would come to an appreciation of Oriental music. The society in which he had been born was eternally valid: the world might grow more sceptical and Christians more

[1] See *Three Russian Prophets*, by Nicholas Zernov (S.C.M.).

withdrawn; but the Coal Age was to be at least millennial, and it would prove impossible to alter.

He is incomprehensible because he did not will that those, other than a trained élite, should comprehend him. His day, which was to be the day of Wagner, Schopenhauer, Nietzsche —and of Ibsen in Scandinavia—thought that it had seen the lasting triumph of technicians over peasants, unmetaphysical sciences over contemplation, and especially of trade-unionism and psycho-analysis over village priestcraft. Life was a series of questions posed to the seat of thinking rather than a totality of racial and spiritual experience, addressed to the senses and the soul. Men who criticized the day itself desired none the less to meet its primary demands. If subtlety were current, their dealings with a hostile world would be more than subtle. It was then, as Spengler points out, that such words as 'hypocrite', 'orthodox', 'heretic', and 'cant' took on a second meaning:

There arises an intellectual art of *playing* with expression, practised by the Alexandrines and the Romantics—by Theocritus and Brentano in lyric poetry, by Reger in music, by Kierkegaard in religion.[1]

Yet, even in the midst of 'play', perhaps unaware that he was doing so—as a child might throw pieces of coloured dulse upon the sand, and be rewarded with a garden—Kierkegaard illuminated truth through the clouds of mere expression:

The story of Abraham then involves a teleological suspension of ethics. As the Individual he has become superior to the universal. This is a paradox which cannot be mediated. It is just as impossible to explain how he enters it as to explain how he remains within it. If this is not the case, then Abraham is not a hero, but a murderer. It is senseless to desire to continue to call him the father of the faith, and to speak of him to men who have no other concern except their concern for words. A man can become a tragic hero by his own strength, but he can never, by his own strength, become

[1] Oswald Spengler: *Decline of the West* (Allen & Unwin).

a knight of the faith. When a man enters what is, in a sense, the difficult path of the tragic hero, there are many who could give him counsel; but when he enters the narrow path of faith, there is no one who can give him counsel, no one who can understand him. Faith is a miracle; yet no one is excluded from it; for passion is common to all men, and faith is a passion.[1]

Such a passage, once it is translated into current terms, must demonstrate the strangle-hold which German philosophy had taken, not only of Danish intellectual thought, but also of the ordinary minds of average Danish people. The Germans unify everything they touch, and everything unified by them will be eventually destroyed. Men's natural reactions, when they are confronted by the mysteries of faith, demand always a 'teleological suspension': that is to say, they see the miracle as being directed to an end, and the phenomenon as impossible to classify until the end is reached. Faith in its early stages— which, when we are considering Christianity, become its *earthly* stages—leads to diversity of outlook. This the Catholic Church can understand; for she has paid a bitter price when she has not understood it. But it cannot be equated with *Kultur*. Three centuries before, *Kultur* had murdered the liturgy in England, offering a 'Common' prayer-book in place of local reverences and habits; it was throttling a sense of wonder and surprise in face of the unknown throughout the North of Europe. From that time onwards, the religious approach was to be consequential.

Kierkegaard had seen this danger, and his chief quarrel with Professor Martensen and Bishop Mynster—men who were leading Church reform from intellectual and theological directions—was on the ground that they had to justify an act of faith before they made it. But there was another peril, so tightly interwoven with the times, that it remained invisible, even from his penetrating genius. Already, in this society driven along furiously by coal, the cult of nerves had become established. An ancient sanity, which used to tell both men and women that they must walk worthily in their different

[1] *Fear and Trembling.*

callings, which acknowledged a variety of equipment but the same Spirit to renew it, had gone with universal dependence on the soil. As *Kultur* was brought to bear upon religion, there was one vocation—sainthood; one method to achieve it —endowment of the Ego with every single gift. If marriage were wrong for any Christian, it were wrong for all; if a knowledge of philosophy were convenient in one case, it must be forced upon the whole communion.

Even in sainthood, an infinite diffusion was rejected. To the German mind sanctity had always seemed too simple. Were not many of the saints quite worldly people? Had not bigotry alone, rather than a perfect faith, impelled them to sacrifice their lives? In the last essence, did not martyrdom itself savour strongly of good works? Kierkegaard saw the ancient piety, but he failed to understand it. In its presence he was a man who reads his *Baedeker* in Chartres Cathedral: he sees the peasants painted upon glass; and they remain dead people, the subjects of dead art.

He had learnt as well that the peculiarly Catholic emphasis on faith was too often an umbrella, sheltering bad morals. Penitents who accused themselves of sins against belief were reprimanded sternly, while those who were guilty of repeated carnal lapses were pardoned, on the ground that their behaviour fell short of their intentions. Despising good works, because to rely on the actions of the body thwarted the movements of the spirit, he was no less distrustful of the ancient *fides*. It led inevitably to an indulgent temper; one which the Reformation had not purged, since it was still alive in the words of Holberg's deacon. One psalm cost so much, and the other so much. . . .

His treatment of Scripture was eclectic, and for him the Incarnation was hardly less dangerous than the life of such a contemporary saint as Bernadette. Before all else, Kierkegaard was a modern townsman. The homely associations of Nazareth and Lourdes, their carpentry and gathering of sticks, their cottage 'cosiness'—never a long way off the naked soil—could be reached too simply and profaned too quickly:

Overcome with emotion you return to those happier times, a sweet and mournful longing leads you to the height of your desires, the desire to see Christ walking in the promised land. You forget the dread and distress and the paradox. Was it easy to avoid making a mistake? Was it not terrible that this man who walked among other men was God? Was it not a terrible thing to sit at table with him? Was it an easy matter to become an apostle? But the result, eighteen centuries of Christianity, that is a help, that has helped on the vile deception by which men deceive themselves and others. I do not feel the courage to desire to be contemporary with such events, and therefore I do not judge severely those who were mistaken, nor do I judge lightly those who saw aright.[1]

If Abraham remained the one figure, eternally safe from human profanation, Kierkegaard's attempt to re-enact his drama in a modern setting delighted the sceptics and dismayed the faithful. It did not, of course, approximate to the original. He never held that this rejection by a plighted man of his betrothed was a test of faith; Regina Olsen was not given to the 'priest' but chosen freely by him; and Regina was sacrificed, not spared. The unhappy incident has been milled so often that neither wheat, nor the germ of wheat, remains; and it should have been possible to dwell on this only as we regard Byron's lameness or the early environment of D. H. Lawrence. Art is a realm wherein the beholders are led frequently to shout: '*O felix culpa!*' O joyful fault, which turned young aristocrat to the writing of great verses; miner's son to the writing of great novels; theologian to the fashioning of lyrics—even though he named them 'dialectical', and meant it. Because he had inflicted pain—the degree was known only to himself, and perhaps only to Regina—he wrote, and could not keep from writing.

Even now the plenitude of his influence has not been established. The Scandinavians in America have made him known; he is read in Germany and Britain, and studied critically in Russia. A group of Spanish Catholics, alive to

[1] *Fear and Trembling.*

the danger of religion's becoming the handmaid of a 'Christian State', place him in the company of Maritain and Georges Bernanos. To all it is increasingly apparent that there is a widening conflict between the unbeliever and the Catholic; that those who possess a Christian faith will adhere more closely to the Church's spirit, although they remain beyond her visible communion. Their nature will be to wish her well, to understand her works of piety, and to thank God for the saints whom she has nourished.

Kierkegaard drew near to this position, but in the eighteen forties it could not have been maintained. Only the advance of time would show how much of modern thought was factual, and how much base interpretation; equally time was essential to convince those outside the Church that she was capable of weathering the journey from a second winter to a second spring. Her future then seemed no less dark than it had done after the sack of ancient Rome. He was preoccupied with present troubles; with the task of saving religious life in Scandinavia; and any question which did not bear instantly upon it seemed merely academic.

He was neither homely, countrified, nor simple. Yet—as it did with Ibsen, in *Peer Gynt* and *The Master Builder*—the land beyond the city shone through his urban setting and experience. One discourse he breaks off to dwell on a small flower, peculiar to the Danish sand-dunes. It is a shy plant; shallow-rooted and quick-growing; thriving best where privacy is granted. Another, to praise a spanking team of horses, whose gloss would vanish soon enough if they were not 'regularly bated. It is at such times that we are glad to rest from the struggle of solving a theological enigma—to acclaim a writer.

SELMA LAGERLÖF

SOMETIMES the pattern of a human life is unfolded inch by inch: sometimes an apparent chance, at one set moment, reveals the whole design. Men have gone to war, from counting-house or coal-mine, and they have returned to serve the community as teachers, or as preachers of religion; others have reached a sudden point at which work in an office at high wages seemed intolerable, and ill-paid work upon the land seemed like very heaven. One or two have told how the call came to them and why it could not be resisted; for the most part the call has been so great a shock that the rest of their lives have been passed in surprised obedience and self-abrogating service. Such people are the bane of lion-hunters and reporters. They are invariably so modest.

If vocation startles some people into silence, a few, here and there, are goaded to talk, and even to talk poetically, of their experience. Florence Nightingale joined this small fellowship when she told of the wounded, haunting her in visions, while she was still safely in her father's house and they were lying out on the Crimea; so did Aloysius Gonzaga when he said that he was a 'piece of twisted iron' which must be straightened out by the discipline of a religious Order; so also did a little schoolteacher in Stockholm when she recounted, years after the event, how she was urged to write the stories which she had heard in childhood. None of these cases suggest a breach of modesty nor anything resembling bad taste: in them all we recognize a feeling of wonder, on the part of ordinary people, that they should have been chosen to perform extraordinary tasks.

The tasks set for Florence Nightingale and Aloysius Gonzaga were seemingly impossible enough: both lived in times when gentle women were expected to follow gentle occupations and when a nobleman was not expected to be noble in a cell; both were told that they were running away from their homes,

72

and so presumably from 'life'; the one was called a traitor
to her sex, and the other a traitor to his class. At first sight
the revolt of Selma Lagerlöf, in favour of the hard and the
heroic, does not appear upon this plane at all: she sacrificed
neither a comfortable home nor a safe job to follow her
vocation; she was never unpopular; and if she was obscure
at the beginning, at the finish she received the public acknowledgment of royalty. The truth is that no sacrifice matters in
itself: what does matter is an agreement to run risks; to stake
everything—even one's last farthing on a tramp or one's last
sheet of paper on a poem.

At stake for Selma Lagerlöf was the good opinion of her
equals. A young schoolteacher, unknown, uninfluential, sent
out a challenge to the great literary men of Scandinavia.
Supposing she had failed. . . . Then the teachers from other
classrooms, the senior girls, aunts, uncles, cousins—all those
who seem to know by telepathy when anyone is 'writing'—
would have called her presumptuous, of course; but their
unkindness would not have ended there; she would have been
made to endure the sly joke and the conspiratorial wink, the
admonition to reverence her betters, the rhetorical question:
"Isn't this work good enough for *you*?"

Her betters were thought to be very good indeed. They
had put Scandinavia upon the literary map of western Europe;
not, so to say, in one colour, but in many: Ibsen's social
plays and Strindberg's problem novels, the critical essays of
Georg Brandes, and the impressionist work of Jonas Lie:
all were accepted by cultured and forward-thinking men, and
it seemed impossible that Scandinavia possessed a further
colour in its spectrum. The future was to show that so many
as five had been retained; colours which were to clash with the
originals; to clash, and put them in the shade.

When Selma Lagerlöf began to write about her childhood,
she shared the general conclusion. For Scandinavian writers
to succeed, they must be bleak as Ibsen, scornful as Strindberg,
and critical as Brandes. It was unlikely that they would attain
to the masters' zenith of perfection: but this was to be their

form, and if they chose another, they would not attain to so much as a middle column in the local weekly. Such problems do confront religious spirits in a pagan age and country-born craftsmen in an age which holds that the only possible material is to be found in cities. For the most part these problems are unsolved, because those who tackle them possess the lion's courage but lack the serpent's guile. They strive to argue pagans into church and city-dwellers to the country: St. Paul made the same attempt in Athens, where he was answered by roars of vapid laughter.

They understand, of course, that a faith cannot be made attractive simply by the use of popular devices. Parsons may show the latest film on a sheet suspended from the roodscreen, or they may adopt a hearty manner from the pulpit; their congregations prefer to see the one in its natural setting, the Astoria, and to hear the other in the genial surroundings of the Dog and Duck. But it is possible to address an age in terms with which that age is otherwise familiar, and to provide religious medicine suitable for contemporary ills. To-day, for instance, when men are suffering from too much isolation—from what has been called 'Suburban Nerves'—it is right and natural that the Church should summon them again to corporate worship, reminding them that the Mass is an action in which the humblest assist. Courage is not lacking, since the very words they use—'worship', 'liturgy', and 'Mass'—have become disreputable terms; yet the courage is nicely mixed with guile; a guile which is obvious common sense.

That is one way to approach the problem; it is the way of the Catholic priest, and increasingly of the Catholic layman also. It is clearly unsuitable for the non-Catholic Christian, who accepts the faith up to a certain point, and after that rejects it. The two people speak a different language: the 'corporate worship' of the one becomes the 'individual experience' of the other, the 'sacrificing priest' becomes a 'preacher of the Gospel', and the 'faithful' become chance members of half-secular societies. Yet the Protestant is not without medicine for the ills of the age in which he lives. He can appeal to a wholly Christian past; he can point out that the age is spending—in the form of public decency and personal kindness—a religious capital which it is taking no steps to replace; and he can create a feeling of nostalgia for days when men believed, and when they behaved as though they did so.

Selma Lagerlöf was a Protestant in Sweden, the most Protestant of European countries. Her crusade, in so far as it was religious, did not urge men to undo the Reformation; it challenged them to make the best of such light as they had been granted. She was nostalgic for a time within memory of her older readers; a time when people sat listening to stories round the fire, accepting the Bible with that love which asks no questions, and walking humbly with God in their several stations. This atmosphere is eighteenth-century and oligarchic; it speaks more of duties than of rights, of being peaceful rather than of being purposeful or zealous, of helping lame dogs over stiles instead of championing a class or dying for the glory of a nation. It is a country atmosphere which pre-supposes the enclosure of common land, the clerical calling as a respectable profession, and the towering of a great house over every village. At the time when Selma Lagerlöf was writing, this was the life led by many people in the more remote provinces of Sweden, while those who had migrated to the towns could still recall it—some with enthusiasm, others with derision.

To the liberal writers it was certainly a sour joke and a monstrous survival. If they thought of the land and the peasantry at all, they thought in terms of improving backward regions and educating backward people. They turned their hard light upon an object, never dreaming that the object could diffuse a soft light of its own. This simile, taken from the introduction which Chesterton wrote to a book by Mary Webb,[1] serves as a reminder that Mary Webb did for an English county, Shropshire, what Selma Lagerlöf did for a Swedish province, Vármland. They were alike, and yet, on the whole, they were very different. Both were country children; both

[1] *The Golden Arrow.*

were Lutheran in outlook, not puritanical but pietistic; both possessed literary styles of great originality, clarity, and beauty. Here comparison must give place to contrast. While Mary Webb wrote of the peasants, making her characters speak for themselves in the Shropshire dialect, Selma Lagerlöf wrote of a different class, putting her own thoughts into their heads, and often her own words upon their lips. While Mary Webb conveys through her books the smell of rain and the sight of an undulating landscape,. now and then frightened from tranquillity by the appearance of a mountain, Selma Lagerlöf shows us frozen lakes whose steely ice will not yield to winter sunlight, and dark forests through which the wolf-packs race after sledges in the hope of human prey. Mary Webb is quiet as the girl who stole away to write her thoughts in the apple-loft at dusk: Selma Lagerlöf is boisterous as the young countess who eloped at midnight with her lover. One goes in search of the light of country things as though it were a flickering candle or a shepherd's lanthorn; the other sits bathed in that same light as though it were the sun which no bricks and mortar can preclude.

Mary Webb was a born writer, in the only sense which should be given to the words. She had no need to cultivate either a public or a style. Writing because she could not help it, she was oblivious to the former and splendidly careless of the latter. If no single publisher had bought her work, the probability is that she would have written six or seven novels —because thinking on paper was the way in which she thought. And it would have been as impossible for her to change her style as it is impossible for a peasant to refrain from digressing, harking back, and pointing copious morals. Just as you must take or leave all peasants, so too you must take or leave born writers.

Selma Lagerlöf was not predestined to her craft: she became what circumstances made her. The first circumstance was poverty: loss of family income and sale of a family estate. She was obliged to train quickly for a suitable profession; and for all the vocation she had received for teaching, she might have become equally well a typist or a nurse. In this alone she was out of sympathy with most contemporary young women; for while they looked eagerly for latch-keys, her one desire was to remain, under parental authority, at home. There, in the seclusion of Márbacka, a Vármland demesne, she would have led nothing resembling the middle-class English version of a secluded life. Vármland was self-contained as Northumberland or Cornwall, not dead and alive as are the counties which depend on London for their education and amusement. For a girl of Selma's class (her people were 'lesser gentry', on good terms with nobility and yeomen, treated with familiar deference by the peasants) there would have been ski-ing, skating, balls, and occasional lectures in the winter, picnics and bathing in the summer, the whole year enriched by happy friendships. It was a well-ordered life, but not by any means a dull one, a place in which you were a foreigner until half a century had passed by since your arrival; a religious culture of which the worst to be said is that it was not cosmic but provincial, and that it neglected modern problems.

The second circumstance which urged Selma Lagerlöf to become a writer was bound up closely with the first. If writing itself was a safety-valve, an escape from the hatefulness of outward things, the material which she used had been given her in Vármland, to guard and cherish wherever life should bring her. Not many years ago (and it must be remembered that Selma Lagerlöf produced her greatest work before the First World War) a girl from Northumberland or Cornwall, driven against her will to London, would have found it natural to re-create on paper the stories which she had heard by word of mouth in childhood. These might have been tales of the Border and the Pilgrimage of Grace, or tales of the smugglers and wreckers; and she would have written them quite literally to pass the time, since the ground had been covered by expert pens already. With the exception of Fröding, whose range was limited to poetic themes, Vármland had not been represented, as the Border was represented by Sir Walter Scott and Cornwall by the Rector of Morwenstowe and Sir Arthur Quiller-Couch. Prior to the Liberal Epoch there were romantics enough in Scandinavia, but their world of romance was artificial as the Hollow Mountain or the Celtic Twilight; not real as a province which is only a few hours away from the capital by train. They made this world, with its trolls and witches, its magic castles, fairy princesses and hobgoblins, because they felt that literature should be more beautiful than life. The contempt which Ibsen and Brandes voiced against them was well merited and overdue. Unless Scandinavian literature went back to reality at once, it would degenerate for all time into pose and polish.

Selma Lagerlöf took this lesson very much to heart. Her first difficulty was to write of a province without being obscurantist; she had therefore to describe people as they were, or as they had been at some time in the course of human history. What may be called her 'Lutheran feeling', her essentially Protestant reaction to social and moral problems, helped powerfully in the choice of time: *Gósta Berling's Saga* was set at the end of the eighteenth century, or in the early nineteenth—in days when men were propelled by horses, when squire and parson reigned supreme in their several districts, and when the State did not attempt to fit square pegs into uniform round holes.

All her pegs were square ones. Gósta himself, an unfrocked preacher; the Major's wife, a mannish, domineering woman, who by sheer will-power drew the last inch of wealth from her estate; Ulrika Dillner, an old housekeeper who ran away from her master because she thought him possessed of the Evil Eye. What could a different society have done with a single one of this wayward, improbable collection? A Fascist, or a Socialist régime, would begin with the praiseworthy idea of putting them to work: Gósta, after a period of probation in a home for inebriates, would be sent to lecture upon the Fallacies of Faith; the Major's wife would be placed in charge of slum mothers or unmarried wives; Ulrika Dillner would be psycho-analysed by a doctor whose specialities were terror and frustration. In a Catholic country they might fare better, but the likelihood is that they would not exist at all; if they did, each would be tolerated, but each would be encouraged, somewhat grimly, to behave: after a few years in monastery and convent, Gósta and the Major's wife (the Church would never waste such a natural prioress on a husband) would return to us, spiritually groomed, thoroughly useful members of society, and not in the very least amusing.

Figures of fun are let loose occasionally upon a Protestant society, both because Protestants lack spheres of utility in which to place them, and also because Lutheran Protestants do not take sin with any degree of seriousness at all. If we turn our minds back to the eighteenth century in England, this will not seem too steep a proposition. There Parson Forde, who luckily left us copious diaries, thought it no sin, but rather a mark of elegance, for a cleric to over-indulge himself at table; at that time the one-bottle man was a milksop and a scandal, while the two-bottle man was a pillar of his class and a gift to his profession. When some squire, reading the lessons with obvious relish on the Sabbath, seduced a village maiden, or drove a carriage up the staircase of his mansion, society might cough in his direction if he abandoned the girl or lamed the horses: the actions in themselves were neither disreputable nor sinful.

Selma Lagerlöf has the typically Lutheran attitude to sin: Lutheran as opposed to Calvinistic, for Calvinist societies, as of Switzerland and Scotland, will not condone breaches of the moral law, and they will not allow greater latitude to the well-born than they vouchsafe to the very poorest. They are egalitarian; Lutheran societies are always oligarchic. Lutherans find it as difficult to believe in sin as they find it easy to make excuses for the sinner. They do not say, as we might expect the Calvinists to do: "This man cannot estrange himself from God, since God has predestined his salvation"; but rather: "This man's actions cannot be too bad, for they are the actions of a believing Christian, and all believing Christians will be saved."

The way of life to which Lutheranism is a contributory factor can be extremely pleasant: the cast of mind which it helps to form is limited, badly equipped, and unresilient. For this faith presupposes, not only a benevolent oligarchy, but a benevolent oligarchy living in the country; not only an acceptance of decent moral standards, but economic circumstances which allow that standard to be kept. When Prussia became a competitive industrial power, Luther's God had to make way for the 'Old German God' of Kaiser Wilhelm; when the Industrial Revolution came about in Britain, the Church of England drew strength from Rome and from Geneva. She may have been as fearful of Newman as she was of Whitfield—the fact remains that they pulled her back to Catholic and Calvinist roots; her Lutheran influences could not cope with the realities of a brutal situation. In Sweden there was the same movement from the country to the towns, although it was more gradual and affected smaller numbers; but there was no alternative religion. Societies which were to become Calvinist had become so finally within a hundred years from the Reformation; they were stern and egalitarian then as they are stern and egalitarian now—Sweden was not destined to be either. Within the Catholic Church, the Counter-Reformation won its victories; but the Jesuits are still precluded from Sweden, where in 1911 a further penal law was passed against all Catholics. To the Swedes religion was and is of the Lutheran variety; its answer to social questions remains government by rank, and to moral questions a quiet life in the country.

There are some questions, particularly moral questions, which it will not face at all. It was this weakness, in the work of Selma Lagerlöf, on which the critics pounced when they wrote: "He who is stupid must be pitied, but pitied the more if he lives in Vármland." The critics recognized that a great city cannot become the focal point for any nation unless that nation is prepared to re-examine each one of its thoughts and feelings and ideas. While they brought up their problems for discussion, only to declare themselves unknowing, religious people, of the Lutheran stamp, would not admit that there were problems to discuss. They tried living in the towns as they had always lived upon the land; when that proved impossible they became nostalgic for old days, well proven ways, and simple people. Selma Lagerlöf voiced their sentiments exactly.

"Oh, children of a later day !" she cried, "I have nothing new to tell you; nothing but what is old and almost forgotten. Tales from the nursery, where the children sit on low stools round the white-haired story-teller, tales from the workmen's kitchen, where the farm labourers and crofters gather about the pine-wood fire . . . talk of the days that are past and gone."

If she shared their sentiments, she shared their reticences also. In her books, amongst the rollicking misfits, male and female, the lovable villains, and the splendidly bad hats, there is enough of human passion, but it is never the passion of desire between the sexes. These people, who are robust in greed and fabulous in pride, become, where love is in question, pale with Lutheran virtue. And the pity is that we cannot believe it. She tries our credulity too hard. The Devil, or his personal agent, we are told, makes an agreement with these decayed gentlemen, these 'Cavaliers', whereby they will live safe and provided in a manor house on the one condition that they do no work other than the Devil's. Up to a point they keep their side of the bargain. The Major's wife, former mistress of the manor, is driven out of doors to beg her bread; the house falls to pieces and the estate is ruined; in the neighbourhood, children are alienated from their parents, and husbands from their wives. Everyone is suitably terrified, but everyone manages to appreciate the joke.

It would be folly to emulate the critics, who analysed *Gósta Berling's Saga* in the twin obscurities of historical ignorance and personal distaste. They said first that there never were such goings on in ancient Vármland, and secondly—even if evidence in support could be produced, that they preferred to doubt it. Mary Webb, writing of a similar place during the

D

same period, introduces us to sin-eaters, local wizards, and young men haunted by the Devil. We take her word for it, not only because memories of the English country live on in the most urban English, but because the sin-eater swallows seduction with the rest, the wizard exposes his daughter naked for reward, and the young man is tempted to abuse the spiritual adoration of his wife. Mary Webb escaped sufficiently from Lutheranism to paint a living picture: Selma Lagerlöf leaves everything from the calling of banns until the baptism of infants to our imagination.

Reading *Gósta Berling's Saga*, one does not doubt the reality of a devil to the Cavaliers, nor their belief that they had made a compact with him: what one is forced to doubt is that he would have fought left-handed, or with a blunted weapon. The suspicion grows that there is some deception; Satan is only half Satanic; and thus the men who war with him, or against him, are rather less than mortal. As he has been exorcized and fumigated to make him fit for Lutheran society, so the Cavaliers have been emasculated. They are quite harmless, they are even lovable; and we are told towards the end that their motives were always of the highest.

Selma Lagerlöf is no more at home with extremes of goodness than she is with extremes of evil. Amongst various legends which have been bound with her book, *The Queens of Kungahálla*, there is one concerning Catherine Benincasa, the girl saint of Siena. This story demonstrates the Lutheran approach to goodness when that approach is both sympathetic and obtuse. Here is a writer going south, away from the environment she knows, it must be feared in search of local colour. And the colour blinds her; blinds her to such an extent that she is unable to distinguish the wood of faith from the trees of cultus, reverence, and affection. It is on this note that the legend opens:

It is in St. Catherine's old house in Siena, a day at the end of April, during the week in which her festival is celebrated. The house with the beautiful balcony and many small rooms, which are now turned into chapels and oratories, in the street of the dyers. Thither people are bringing bouquets of white lilies, and the scent of incense and violets hangs about the house. While they do so, they say to themselves, "It seems just as though the little Catherine were quite recently dead and as though those who are going in and out of her house had seen and known her." But, as a matter of fact, no one can believe that she is dead, for in that case there would have been more grief and lamentation, not merely a quiet sense of regret. It seems rather as though a beloved daughter had been just married and taken away from her father's house. . . .

And it is almost on this other note that the legend ends. St. Catherine has been striving for the conversion of Nicola Tunga, a young nobleman condemned to death.

"Before you came," she said, "I placed my neck on the block in order to see if I could bear it, and I felt that I still have a dread of death and that I do not love Jesus well enough to be willing to die this hour. Nor do I wish you to die, and my prayers have no power." As she said this, he thought, "If I had lived I should yet have won her." And he was glad that he would die before he had dragged down the bright bride of Heaven to the earth. But when he laid his head in her hands, there came to them both a great comfort. "Nicola Tunga," she said, "I see Heaven opening. Angels are hovering about in order to receive your soul." . . .

It is a rare phenomenon for Lutherans to sense the attractiveness of Catholic ceremonial and devotion. In *Gósta Berling's Saga* there is a chapter describing a Vármland church, whose whitewash, as well as the disappearance of plaster saints, Selma Lagerlöf is ready to deplore. One feels that she yearns for the trappings of a drama, but that the drama itself must contain no tragic scenes; and for the Christian Faith, provided that its central fact, a cross, has been removed. Under her hand St. Catherine becomes, not so much a saint, as an extraordinary young woman; a girl whose character was always quite unusual, requiring no preparation for its final renunciation of the world. In the first place, Selma Lagerlöf doubted the efficacy of the Catholic training to sainthood—

confession, Holy Communion, constant prayer, and continual self-humiliation; and in the second, she would not admit that the world was a foe to be renounced. As the Cavaliers meant well, so also did the world; as their motives were always of the highest, equally high were the motives of worldly people. Because a Lutheran public could not bear hard facts, they were shown a saint who might have been a daughter of the local manse: she had a sweet disposition, she was given to good works, and, if she had taken a vow of chastity, that was at worst a personal foible.

The vow of chastity was the one thing which made St. Catherine a remarkable person, and which made her memory enduring. Had she refrained from this sacrifice, which the least of them could understand at once, the burghers of Siena, always frugal and suspicious, would not have wasted their money on candles in her honour nor their time on visiting her house. Selma Lagerlöf, and still more her Swedish readers, might understand the sacrifice of sex, but they could not tolerate the renunciation of romance. Therefore the story of a great love, the love of a soul for its Creator, becomes a love story with an unhappy ending. Had Nicola's life been spared, he would have won her. This is so improbable that we are forced from the world of fact into a world of fiction, and from the contemplation of a character to the mere witnessing of puppets. As the Cavaliers fail because they are too good, St. Catherine fails because she is not nearly good enough. Both are shown to us through Lutheran eyes: eyes which are restless but rather vague, kind but extremely sentimental.

Selma Lagerlöf is sometimes attracted to the South, yet only in the North, and only there in times since the Reformation, is she happy as a writer. Her full-length portrait of St. Olav is no more true to life and history than is her thumbnail sketch of the Italian virgin. Here again austerity must yield pride of place to high romance; for we are shown Queen Astrid winning the tough warrior with a feminine guile which barely escapes from being coquettish. Of Catholics in modern Scandinavia she makes no single mention, leaving Sigrid

Undset to answer questions of the day on their behalf, through the voice, and through the personality still more, of Father Harold Tangen. She remains within her chosen limits; Lutheran limits which exclude democracy, Socialism, divorce, the urban poor, and which should exclude both the South of Europe and any time—to take two England landmarks—before the abdication of James Stuart or after the accession of Victoria.

It is almost as difficult for us to sum up her literary achievement as it was for Brandes, and the other Scandinavian critics, when they first read *Gósta Berling's Saga*. Because we do not share their view of progress, granting an evolutionary character to history—primitive, medieval, modern; uphill all the way, with a mechanical El Dorado at the top—we shall not regard her as one who wilfully fell back. She was no more reactionary than are whole cultures, and the individual nations which compose them, when they react against a wrong ascent, feeling that it can take them nowhere, and return to a point at which the ways divided. Perhaps she did not return quite far enough; perhaps the Lutheran atmosphere was not an air in which great art could flourish. Certainly it possessed small consolation for those who had entered El Dorado, only to find it an accursed city of the plains.

Yet, if we pronounce these heavy judgments, we shall be taking her too seriously; far more seriously than she herself intended. She was romantic, but we cannot call her a Romantic; she taught school to earn a living, but to think of her as naïve, or over-innocent, or 'missish' would be to study a shadow without once glancing at the figure from whom it was reflected. She was not a born writer in the sense that writing was her obvious vocation: she was a medium to whom the stories whispered: "We must be told: please tell us!" And to have it in this way is to have the better part.

When in the Listening Time, before all two-legged creatures had a smattering of letters, the minstrels went from castle to castle, or from cave to cave, they were bent, not upon errands of instruction, but upon errands of mercy and of mirth. They

made men forget the darkness, made them chuckle deep in the
solar plexus, and sometimes laugh aloud. Here is Selma
Lagerlöf's tradition. As the old minstrels dispelled the gloom
of isolated dwellings, this new one lifts the grey coal-fog a
little from the streets. We, 'children of a later day', huddling
of a winter's afternoon against the central heating or the gas,
with Gósta for company and the world shut out beyond the
curtains, may know the delight of pine-wood fires and of a
white-haired story-teller close beside us. We are in no need
then to be censorious. If it is all a little improbable, does that
matter greatly? The Cavaliers are lovable, why spoil them by
asking social questions and setting ethical conundrums? They
were too busy at being alive to give us satisfactory answers.

Then, if we allow this mood to settle, we shall begin to see
the truth which is above hard facts, and the glow which is
more warming and revealing than hard light; the glow which
radiates from the midst of country legends. With that knowledge, we shall pass quite painlessly from entertainment to
instruction, and from instruction to the drawing of a moral.
What should the moral be? Selma Lagerlöf refused point-
blank to tell us. Tolerance, it might have been, or the art
of living with our neighbours, or possibly reverence for tradition.
But if she were here, and if we pressed her to reply, she, who
loved everything home-made, would answer: "The best is
drawn by each one for himself, because he can draw no other."

THE AGNOSTIC

J. P. JACOBSEN

DIALECTICAL progression is not by any means confined to the changing order of society. It is the metaphysic, for example, which underlies all work upon the land, where the ploughing of winter is done so that spring growth may not be impeded, and even crops are hurried home lest they delay the breaking up of stubble until the rain or frost prevents it. In literature we find that one genius is not waiting to grasp his predecessor's mantle, or one 'school' waning just as another waxes. There is rather interplay of thought and interpolation of deductions. Each proposal calls forth its natural opposition, and each arrival holds the germ of its departure. Moments dawn when a true artist knows his feelings, and when he can bear no longer to nourish them in silence. We say that a prevailing mood has 'stung' him into action.

True everywhere and all the time, this progression is illustrated most perfectly in the literature of Scandinavia. Ibsen and Strindberg worked throughout a mental phase which took for granted, not only the Evangelical approach to Christian revelation, but also the permanence of 'saga values': personal heroism, national optimism, and the endowment of Nature with human ·sentiments and feelings. Yet, after their work had been produced, positions were gradually reversed. Now scepticism and pessimism came into circulation, while the Christian virtues seemed old-fashioned and outmoded. The process began, but it was allowed no respite. As Ibsen denied mankind's dependence upon a supernatural order, Kierkegaard affirmed that this dependence must increase with technical ingenuity, and that it must keep pace with human progress: as they both, from different angles, made mirth at the expense of Lutheran ideals, Selma Lagerlöf took these same ideals under the multi-coloured cloak of her romances. Music,

87

although desiring to be an arbiter and neutral, could not remain outside the spiritual arena. It was Grieg who saved the Liberal writers from despair, and Sibelius who produced 'cold water' when the artistic gullet had been rendered almost insatiable by 'cocktails'.

The two Protestants strove to perform a common task, but they had no personal trait in common. The Danish philosopher was every inch a realist; sophisticated, at home in the polished world of Copenhagen, and always able to maintain his European contacts. The Swedish novelist inherited the tradition of early nineteenth-century romantics: wide-eyed and open-hearted, she was never blasé for a moment, since she detested Stockholm and adored her native province with an equally captivating zest. The ultimate purpose of these artists was the same; but had they met, they would have bored each other to distraction. No slighter temperamental cleavage separated Jacobsen from Brandes, Ibsen, and those whom we associate with the Bohème of Christiania.[1] Indeed, it is doubtful if he can be called a Liberal writer. The rest of them were working consciously for social, political, and above all for feminist reforms: he had no interest in 'Questions of the Day', since his view precluded the assumption that mere change would improve a rotten order. On the ground of dis- belief—disbelief in,

> . . . a divinity that shapes our ends,
> Rough-hew them how we will,

he was ready to identify himself with the Bohème. In this they were agreed, and to spread agnosticism was their mutual purpose.

Although these men were not contemporaries in the stricter sense, they belonged to that epoch which regarded humanity in terms of natural and inevitable progress. They were at one in Scandinavia as Bennett, Wells, and Galsworthy were at one in Britain; Joyce the Irishman, Kafka the Hungarian, and

[1] An artistic coterie in Oslo during the two decades before Norwegian Independence—i.e., prior to 1905.

Sigrid Undset the Norwegian had yet to clothe in words a Europe-wide suspicion that the cultural barometer was falling.

Jacobsen's method, however, was solitary and individual. It was not that the other Liberals worked before the emergence of Darwinian science, and Jacobsen much later; it was rather that he alone amongst them could grasp, immediately and fully, the significance of evolution. They might have said: "We *feel* the Christian thesis to be wrong. Darwin, no doubt, has contributed some sound proofs." He did say: "I know Darwin to be right, and therefore Christianity *is* wrong."

For Ibsen the emotional argument had a strong appeal. The more he pondered human maladjustments—in homes and offices, and in the breakdown of cabinet diplomacy—the more certain he became that a God "Who is a supreme Spirit, Who alone exists of Himself, and is infinite in all perfections" would not tolerate such evils. Putting aside the Wellsian possibility of a weak, disinterested, or wholly impotent Creator, an inverted Humanism of this kind does lead cultivated men to become Agnostics. Jacobsen, on the other hand, saw man in due perspective. There were other orders. Invertebrates and subhuman vertebrates; microscopic plants and tiny particles of fungus: the facts governing their lives and histories did not appear to tally with the Christian revelation, and therefore the deposit of truth must have been erroneous. Of all the Liberal writers, he was the least pragmatic; he neither bent nor garnished a supposed reality to make his thoughts more tolerable or the universe more cheerful. His contribution to the sum total of despair must have been tremendous. . . .

We cannot examine such a craftsman unless we are prepared to admit that he was working in good faith. Once allow a suspicion as to his honesty of purpose, and he has been degraded from the rank of genius. There is no ground on which to doubt him. Yet there is every reason why we should look more closely at the data from which, a half-century ago, he drew such shattering conclusions. And a knowledge of the evidence is not in itself sufficient for a judgment. The scene has vanished, and the evidence is therefore circumstantial.

We labour under those hardships which beset a young barrister, reading the famous trial at which his father spoke for the defendant. There is the same judge, the same counsel on both sides, the same witnesses, for the prisoner and against him, the same twelve jurors nodding in their box. Yet this young man finds that the scene has been transplanted from reality to history. It has no life. It is purely static. Where are the intonations of men's voices? The inexplicable hiatus? The guilty pause? The still more guilty torrent of invective? He must learn, as we must, to go along without them.

The Christian apologists of Jacobsen's own day are gone beyond the reach of bailiffs and subpœnas. We discover them in books, subject to a double limitation—of fiction, and of a fiction which has become outmoded. Here, then, is a pastor, Mr. Bigum:[1]

. . . Mr. Bigum . . . was not one who could lead a soul back to the old paths. Indeed his temperamental philosophy, by virtue of which he could be fired and enraptured by each and every side of the question—to-day, one; to-morrow, another—set all dogmas adrift in the minds of his pupils. At bottom he was really a man of Christian principles, and if anyone could have pinned him down to saying what was the fixed point in all this fluid matter, he would most likely have replied that it was the creed of the Evangelical Lutheran Church or something akin to that, but he himself had very little inclination to drive his pupils along the straight road of orthodoxy or to warn them at every step that the least deviation from the beaten track meant straying into lies and darkness, likely to end in perdition and hell; for he had none of the passionate concern of the orthodox for jots and tittles. He was in fact religious in the slightly artistic, superior manner such talented people affect, not afraid of a little harmonizing, easily enticed into half-conscious rearrangements and adaptations, because, whatever they do, they must assert their own personality, and, in whatever spheres they fly, must hear the whirring of their own wings.

Such people do not guide, but their instruction has a fullness, a copiousness, and a wobbly many-sidedness which, provided they do not utterly confuse a pupil, tend to develop his independence

[1] *Neils Lyhne*, by Jens Peter Jacobsen (Cambridge University Press).

in a high degree, since they almost force him to make up his mind
for himself. . . .

It was this limited equipment which Mr. Bigum brought to
the task of educating young Neils Lyhne—a receptive and
highly imaginative pupil. The Lutheran pastorate of that
generation resembled La Fontaine in his twenties. One day
La Fontaine was riding home with certain 'documents, on
which the fate of an inheritance depended, slung loosely from
his saddle; he did not know that he had let them fall, for
when a postilion galloped up and offered him a mud-stained
packet, he at first disowned it. This was the exact predicament
of the Scandinavian Churches. Carrying a treasure—the
Christian revelation—the value of which they had never
troubled to assess, they let it fall, and then denied that it had
been put into their keeping. Transubstantiation gave way to
Consubstantiation, Consubstantiation to a vaguer 'Presence';
whereupon the Presence, and even the 'historical Jesus', was
tacitly rejected. After a few years of Mr. Bigum, it is not
surprising that Neils was tender meat for the Copenhagen
vultures. A young doctor waylays him on Christmas Eve, and
puts Atheism to him as a persecuted minority-opinion:

"Have you noticed that most of the idealistic forces in our
country, and probably the best of them, are entirely absorbed in
the cause of political freedom? You can take a lesson from that.
Believe me, there is saving grace in fighting for an idea that is
gaining ground, but it is very demoralizing to a man to belong
to a losing minority, which life, in its inevitable course, puts in the
wrong, point by point, step by step. It cannot be otherwise, for
it is bitterly disheartening to see that which your inmost soul
believes to be right and true, to see this Truth reviled and struck
in the face by the meanest camp-follower in the victorious army,
to hear her called vile names, while you can do nothing at all except
to love her even more faithfully, kneel to her in your heart with
even deeper adoration, and see her beautiful face as radiantly
beautiful as ever and as full of majesty, shining with the same
immortal light, no matter how much dust is whirled up around her

white forehead, no matter how thickly the poisonous fog closes in around her halo. . . ."[1]

Although this portrait does not belong to one Northern country more than to another, it is clearly dated. Nowadays men do not kneel to Atheism in their hearts; they do not endow her with a face—still less with a face that is 'radiantly beautiful'; nor do they think that she shines with an 'immortal light'. Modern disbelief, even when it is radical and total, is presented as a counsel of despair. The unbeliever—who would in any case call himself 'agnostic'—regards religious faith in terms of a definite acquisition. This he would be happy to possess, but either the facts of life seem to tell against it, or else his personal apathy prevents him from weighing up the evidence on either side. He will do so later on—when his wealthy uncle dies, or he retires from business, or grows weary of his mistress. The atmosphere is never heated, and the salient point is that the Agnostic believes there to be an equally strong case—for religion and against it.

Yet we need not go back very far in history to find a battle raging throughout the light literature of England, no tamer than the one which Jacobsen began in Denmark. Naturally some allowances must be made for language. People in books by Wells and Hardy were gifted with a sense of humour (though it was always grim and sometimes pawky) to match the characters of Chesterton and Mary Webb. Being English, they used the word 'soul' on very rare occasions, while the Danes, for their part, obviously enjoyed it. Subject to this, we meet Wells's urban scoffers and Hardy's rural doubters as serious individuals. They did not suppose for a moment that there were two sides to the religious question, nor that the arguments for faith equalled those against it. There might be a 'President of the Immortals'; if so, he had created the world, only to sleep on his achievement.

What has happened between the end of last century and the present day to effect this alteration? First, we are living

in an age which is altogether less concentrated in its approach
to abstract questions. The necessity for dealing with global
wars, followed by unemployment, trade-depression, and
inflation has speeded sideways progress and stunted upwards
growth. While technics have flourished, theology has inevitably
withered. Politics in turn have become a branch of technics.
Idealistic forces *have* been absorbed in the cause of political
freedom, since only the certainty of tangible results seem
worthy of their efforts. Things quantitative make a deep
impression: things qualitative tend to be ignored. It is signifi-
cant that when the Archbishop of Canterbury (Dr. Temple)
was answering a layman's difficulties on the wireless, the whole
argument was based on solid cash. Instead of discussing the
Incarnation, the Resurrection, and the Judgment, they discussed the Archbishop's salary, and how he ought to spend it.
Fifty years ago this could not have happened. Because the
power of money was unchallenged, man's economic present
could be brushed aside for his celestial future. Mr. Bigum's
spirit—harmonizing, adapting, rearranging—has therefore come
into his own, and he himself would be ordained, at least in the
Protestant denominations, with very little trouble. In 1890
he was still a noticeable charlock in the cornfield.

Mere inertia on the one hand and mere adaptation on the
other do not answer our original question. The human mind
may be shifted in fits and starts from a contemplation of the
Four Last Things: it will always come home to them in the
presence of national calamity or personal disaster. When one
dies, the rest know that they must follow: this knowledge
separates mankind from waking animals and from sleeping
vegetation. Yet a dwelling upon eternal truths is easily dis-
turbed. In Jacobsen's generation, for example, both Atheists
and Christians were diverted by a passing phase of science,
and both believed that it had barred the way, permanently,
to a final peace between them. One thought that Darwin had
spoken the last word concerning the origin of species; the other,
that this 'last word' was diametrically opposed to revelation.

The nineteenth century, helped along by philosophical

Liberalism, which was its own unique creation, saw itself standing on the top rung of a cultural ladder. It believed that the past could contribute nothing useful to the present; or at least that past achievements, in art and in the art of living, existed for ornament, and not for imitation. While the French Revolution was the beginning of materialism, spirituality was rooted in the German Reformation. When Darwin appeared, each side saw *The Origin of Species* in its limited perspective. For Christians this was an agonizing process. Luther had taught *fiducia*—blind trust, not *fides*—reasoned faith, an inevitable warfare between natural and supernatural knowledge —never the possibility of establishing a synthesis between them. The Christian answer to Darwinian science was not the only untenable opinion. If the Christians pretended that Old Testament chronology was true—come what might, speak to the contrary who dared !—the materialists forgot that biology was growing. Before long it would have grown sufficiently mature to dispute its own conclusions. But it was young enough when Jacobsen produced *Neils Lyhne*, and he was able to enjoy the popularity of one who had struck a cunning blow for human enlightenment and progress.

The spirit of this conflict outlasted Jacobsen by no more than twenty years, and it is now so dated that we are able to describe it as 'Victorian', or 'Edwardian', or 'Prior to the First Great War'. A challenge, having the inevitable strength of action planned, delayed, and reasoned, was voiced from post-war pulpits; and not from them alone, since the 'advanced' thought of yesterday had become, as it always must, the retrogression of to-day. No longer could agnostic science have first claim upon the public, for men whose lungs had been destroyed by phosgene were less credulous than their fathers, who had gazed in wonder at the marvels of X-ray. They suspected their own cleverness and the good intentions of humanity in general; Bernard Shaw condensed the mood on paper when he wrote, "neo-Darwinism consists for the most part of grossly unscientific statements of superstitious nonsense".

The opposition came from many quarters. If the Catholic Church, having delivered itself of startling pronouncements on the theme of social justice, felt able to turn from man's present and future to his less clamorous beginnings, there was a High-Church movement in the English-speaking world which had been studying these questions, behind locked doors, for close on fifty years. Again, a new type of humanism was abroad; a humanism which showed its limitations at Geneva, but had the wisdom to believe that man was a free agent and the master of his fate.

Each opponent of agnostic science disputed the necessity of continued warfare between Christianity and Darwinian evolution. Studying the ancient Fathers in search of a theological eirenicon, Oxford scholars found that a working hypothesis had been suggested by St. Gregory of Nyssa to the early Church. On this scientific data were to be examined, as and when they came to light in the course of history. It declared, first that God laboured generally through an instrumental cause, constructing the instrument to achieve the end in view; secondly that God had created by a single act an unformed universe of matter containing in itself all the varied and harmonious details that we now see, and that their development or evolution took place according to the natural physical laws which He had Himself instituted.[1]

The reason why neither Jacobsen nor the Christians of his time could grasp this explanation is that they were too arrogant in their approach to history. The Protestant world did not dream of turning to the ancient Fathers for illumination until Newman had forced their books into the open. Then, however, two sides of the Christian opposition were able to converge. Hitherto, ever since the Reformation, there had been an absolute religious cleavage between the North and South of Europe. In Denmark, as in England, Protestants felt simply that no good thing could come from the Eternal City. The Roman Church itself had met the New Learning with the

[1] See Philip de Ternant: *Some Pathfinders of Organic Evolution* (Burns, Oates. 1928).

Counter-Reformation— a stern-tempered and rigidly dogmatic
movement. By 1900, with the dawning of an 'Œcumenical'
outlook, views had been exchanged. The natural method was
for Protestants and Catholics to go back, beyond the date of
their historic quarrel, in search of a common ancestry and a
common inspiration. From Gospel times they moved to the
Patristic Era, where they encountered St. Gregory of Nyssa.

The Catholic emphasis, of course, has always been placed
upon salvation—sometimes to the exclusion of speculative
thinking. Yet this may be a safeguard; for where no pronouncements have been made, the Faithful are at liberty to draw their
own inferences from available material. Catholicism was on
the whole well armed for this adventure. While the Belgian
scientist Lamarck, himself *pratiquant* and acquainted with the
Fathers, had established the distinction between vertebrates
and invertebrates, and had abolished Aristotle's ladder-
diagram of life's stages, substituting the accepted diagram of a
tree with branches, Mendel, the Augustinian abbot, had
initiated the science of genetics.

This meeting of Protestants and Catholics in defence of their
religion took place many years after the publication of *Neils
Lyhne*. At that time there seemed to be at most two types of
Christian: the one narrow, obstinate, triumphant; the other,
personified by Mr. Bigum, "easily enticed into half-conscious
rearrangements". Knowing that the first would require a
sacrifice of intellect, and the second of integrity, Jacobsen
gave battle to them both. In doing so he was forced to scorn
the Gospel. . . .

Now the very argument which Atheists, or Agnostics,
advance most commonly against religion—that religious people
do not live up to their professions—shows an acceptance of
the principle that actions are prompted by beliefs. If this
were not so, the argument would have no meaning. The
World would say to Christians, in effect: "You love Jesus and
venerate the saints, but you are not expected to follow their
example." This thought is never uttered. Amongst Buddhists,
the World looks for a reflexion, however pale, of Buddha;

amongst Mohammedans, of Mohammed; amongst Christians, of Jesus Christ. Therefore, when a man shoulders the obligation of kneeling to Atheism in his heart, we are entitled to examine his subsequent behaviour in the light of his profession. If his actions are found to be good, noble, and creative, we may say —It was so, in spite of his beliefs—just as we should say (of the immoral Buddhist, Mohammedan, or Christian)—It was so, in spite of his.

Jacobsen, however unwittingly, maintained this principle quite fully—for *Neils Lyhne* is a psychological study in disintegration. In the first place hereditary mutations are allowed to play their part. The boy's mother is a dreamer, an idealist, a luxury which yeoman stock tolerates once in every generation —so long as the exotic growth be female. His father, on the other hand, is a decadent aristocrat and an unconscious actor. When they have been wedded for some time, the woman discovers that the man has fooled her:

> She sank back into the dreams of her girlhood, but with the difference that they were now no longer illuminated by hope. . . .

After Neils was born these factors ceased to count as heredity and they became environment; but, in either case, the embryonic disaster was apparent: hopeless dreams, a bitter couple, and a lonely child between them.

This phenomenon—of a lonely child, the one fruit of dreary wedlock—has since become a trade-mark which distinguishes the psychological romance from books whose purpose is instruction, entertainment, or conversion. It is a necessary 'prop'. Not only are psychopaths comparatively rare amongst large families—where the corners of one are rubbed off by the sharpening plane-blade of the others—but these large families are themselves so rare in the modern world that a novelist could not portray them without doing violence to the facts of history. Jacobsen was ahead of his time, a pioneer; and it was essential for his purpose that young Neils should have been solitary so far back as memory could take him.

For Neils, as for all the solitary children of our European winter, outside contacts are of huge importance. He is a stranger to that robust exclusiveness, that fraternal comradeship, that sense of the home as a strong tower against the world which we find during agrarian periods and amongst prolific peoples. A 'feeling introvert', he must speculate in childhood whether some playmate returns his full affection, and in adolescence whether he is 'worthy' of some fellow-student. Such characters have been drawn since then by Flaubert, Dostoevski, Charles Morgan, Richard Aldington—in their different times and countries.

The fact that this book has not been banned shows the insoluble problem of a wise censorship on moral grounds. No description of carnal intercourse between the sexes rivals in lubricity Jacobsen's unerring choice of the evil setting and the diabolical suggestion. Pornography, dealing with the existence and fulfilment of natural desires—even when seduction is the theme, holding it up as an amusing weakness—does not teach that virtue is essentially vicious, and vice a synonym for virtue. Moralists are apt to exaggerate its perils, since they forget that it does not teach at all.

Pornography, however, can never be a practicable guide to mental health, and it is well to judge a craftsman by his equals. A quotation, taken more or less at random from the novels of Hugh Walpole, will serve to show how sexual evil impinges upon the Christian mind:

He seemed to her a man really possessed, in literal fact, by devils. . . . He pretended to glory in his narration, boasting and swearing what he would do when he returned to the old scenes, how happy and triumphant he had been in the midst of his filth—but young and ignorant though she was she saw beneath this the misery, the shame, the bitterness, the ignominy. . . . She saw many foreign countries and many foreign towns, and in them all men and women were evil. . . . The things that these inhabitants did were made quite plain to her. She saw the dancing-saloons, the women naked and laughing, the men drunken and besotted, the gambling, the quarrelling, drugging, suicide—all under a half-dead sky. . . . "Martin," she cried, "don't let's be so serious about it. You *can't* want to go back to that life—it's so dull. At first I was frightened, but now!—why it's all the same thing over and over again." . . .[1]

Maggie Cardinal was not injured by hearing the worst of sexual vice, because a perverse moral judgment did not give the verdict in its favour. When Fennimore is seduced by Neils —Neils who was her husband's greatest friend—they are blamed only for concealment:

> There was no change. At least there was no return to the former days, but the flabby uncleanness of living as they did and not running away together became more present in their consciousness and linked them together in a closer and baser union through the common sense of guilt; for neither of them wished any change in things as they were. Nor did they pretend to each other that they did. . . .[2]

In spite of every depraved action and tormenting thought which had flowed quite naturally from his acceptance of the Atheist *mystique*, Neils could not see why he should reject it. The disaster of Fennimore only developed self-assurance, since he leaves her to marry a young girl, whose faith he undermines with relish. Throughout he is a Modern Man, the urban intellectual; ignorant and clever, artistic and uncultured, terrified of suffering unless it is he who inflicts pain upon his friends and lovers. Then, of course, it is held to have a very chastening effect.

If circumstances had not been working in his favour, Jacobsen would have known that fate which is the normal recompense for slow, deliberate writing: a niche but not a pinnacle, local and limited success, but never international fame. The doctor in *Neils Lyhne* might speak of atheism as the minority and the trampled opposition, of Christians as secure, established, and triumphant; yet this was quite untrue. A secular approach to life, rationalizing metaphysics and the arts until what little remained of them could agree with Darwin's thesis, rationalizing technics, with which sociology was henceforward to be numbered, was well in the ascendant. Jacobsen moved

[1] *The Captives.*   [2] *Neils Lyhne.*

with a victorious army. His companions, both aesthetes and intellectuals, relied on him for that special knowledge which they had never troubled to acquire. His profound ignorance of the early Fathers, of Mendel and Lamarck, did not count against him. Only now do scientists approach with caution the age which mistook a growing, groping study for a 'Novum Organum' of established truth. Yet in Scandinavia his memory is cherished with a deep affection. A rebel against their powerful Church, and therefore—as it stands in Lutheran countries—against the dual authority of crown and mitre, he is seen as the 'little man', the eternal David picking up smooth pebbles, to hurl them at Goliath. But the events of to-day are forcing the Scandinavians to ask an awkward question: "What will David give us, when he has slain Goliath?"

Although prophecy is dangerous, and there are a variety of answers to the question, we have seen at least that one tyranny is substituted for another. Furthermore, the particular freedom which one man especially desires is the first tyranny which he will be guided to enforce. Those who held that religion was the 'opium of the people' dosed the people with dialectical materialism; those who liberated States from the party system, compelled allegiance to a single party with the help of rubber truncheons; even in the comparatively harmless matter of good writing, pioneers who freed us from the hated colon insist that we should hail the brown-shirted asterisk, their leader. Jacobsen's tyranny is obvious. He would have bound the world to unpleasant passion. Unpleasant? In its stricter meaning—yes. To a monotonous lust, in the fulfilment of which there would not be the very smallest pleasure. Living at a time when the dignity of natural love had escaped from its rightful place in the Christian message—it was in that century marriage became 'a rather wicked sacrament'—Jacobsen was taught to regard it as profane. To pursue him farther must be to follow a man into the desert. His thirst will grow, his loneliness increase; and we are only wise, in a world where there is futility enough, if we refuse point-blank to go beside him on a sleeveless errand.

THE NATIONALISTS

VERNER VON HEIDENSTAM

WHEN a man is told that he fights 'for democracy' or 'to make the world safe for democracy', he is generally suspicious and resentful. The word has been used too often. It has become a 'witch word', meaning one thing on the lips of a mine-owner, a newspaper proprietor, or a millionaire, and something quite different on the lips of a skilled worker, a small trader, or a sweep. To one group it may imply the right to live in luxury on unearned income, and to the next a possibility of living in subhuman quarters, on starvation wages, and of grumbling against them without being tortured by the police. Each man translates the word according to his mental habits and his habits of life. It may produce any of the following reflexes, and many more beside them. Democracy: They can't pinch me for what I haven't done. Democracy: The State must allow me a reasonable profit from my business. Democracy: I can send my children to a denominational school. I can let off steam in Hyde Park. I can kiss any girl who'll let me.

The weakness of these associations is that they are all rights, while ordinary experience tells us that the law of life is based on give and take. Wages are paid for services performed; the land yields its crops after careful cultivation; children respect their parents because the parents have sacrificed wealth and leisure to sustain them. But it is not this separation of democracy from natural and inevitable duties which makes the soldier angry. He knows full well that the duties are implied, and that he must behave in a certain way in order to benefit from an enlightened social system. What does arouse his anger is the political habit of 'cornering' superior ideals to serve inferior ends.

If "every child born into this world alive is either a little Liberal or a little Conservative", we cannot prove it from

political examples. "Whatever is of good repute, either on
my left or on my right, that will I claim and turn to personal
profit." . . . Such is the backbone, the pith and spleen, of all
political addresses. But in literature, where men reveal their
inner hearts more slowly and more truly, we can find proof that
humanity is roughly cleft in two on its approach to social issues.
Ibsen was at least some kind of 'little Liberal'; Verner von
Heidenstam possessed the mental habits of a young Conservative
throughout his working life.

The qualifying adjective is of great importance. Heidenstam
was not a Tory. The term 'Tory' should connote belief in a
close relationship between the Church as spiritual legislative
and the State as secular executive—an impossible position for
one who never called himself a Christian. He was not an
Imperialist: Sweden neither sought nor gained an empire;
the extent of her territorial ambitions, long since dead in any
case, was to dominate the Baltic Sea. If he falls into that
grouping which we have come to call the 'Right' this fact does
not enable us to bless or curse him. It is a good point from
which to begin a careful study.

During the 1880's Heidenstam and Strindberg held a series
of more or less formal conversations which Strindberg recorded
in his diary. Heidenstam's family were iron-masters in the
North of Sweden, and he told Strindberg that there had been
disputes, disturbances, and bloodshed. Then he said: "We
are too cultured or too weak to employ the same forms of
barbarism as they do: we will go under, and with us culture
itself." A most revealing statement!—especially so since the
thought behind it is a thoroughly normal Young Conservative
approach to social problems. (Not a settled philosophy or
considered outlook: a beginning, a departure, a sudden awareness of dragon's teeth sown between the classes.) Dissecting
it, we find these implications:—First: culture, thought, and
intellect presuppose an inability to deal ruthlessly with a
ruthless foe. Secondly: the uncultured, those who work with
their hands for meagre wages, are naturally barbaric. Thirdly:
if the class from which the Young Conservative is drawn

'goes down', everything of value must necessarily 'go down' with it. Fourthly: the disaster is inevitable and cannot be prevented: "We *will* go down, and with us culture itself." Here is a decadence of the Right which fully equals that decadence of the Left which we associate with Jacobsen the Dane —Heidenstam's contemporary and polaric opposite. Jacobsen held that the Western World was doomed. The thought did not distress him: the Western theme, its binding agency, religion, was exploded; and that which had been held together by a falsehood would do well to vanish. Heidenstam's despair was on account of things which he could love—patriotism, privilege, a man's right to endow his children; a world bereft of them would not be fit to live in. This decadence of the Right has a parallel in modern France: there the followers of Flandin, and later of Laval, would not fight for the French State: it was no longer *their* State; since it had been given to the workers.

A session of the Brains Trust was asked whether all great achievements—literary, musical, artistic—owed their inspiration to personal anguish, or at least to the dwelling of those who created them in an anguished world. But the answer was not satisfactory; the sufferings of Milton and of Dante were quoted to support the thesis, and Browning's happy life was quoted to refute it. The word 'conflict' must have trembled on many tongues that evening. Conflict is not of necessity a thing of pain: it is the tinder and the flint, the spark and flame, the keen air which beats on the artist's brow, forcing him to greatness. A man need not suffer more than his fellows do to be articulate when they are silent; but he must feel causes deeply, experience beauty strongly, and sense that opposition which is always willing the destruction of *his* cause and the spoliation of his private beauty. Once this happens, good work is sure to flow, since it is the involuntary response to a law of human nature.

Our difficulty, both as critics and students of such work, lies in maintaining a neutrality towards the writer's cause so that we may lose nothing in our appreciation of his writing. Here adult education may render a service in striking contrast to that disservice which is rendered by the Book Clubs. For how pitiful it is when culture comes to such a pass that so-called 'men of culture' can bear to read only those opinions with which they are already in agreement! Their vision then is restricted to the particular conflict which their chosen authors have experienced: the conflict of religious spirits in a questioning society; of the proletariat with established and traditional order; of the traditionalist with a world which finds his certainties outworn. This difficulty will be overcome when we can approach every conflict with detachment; thanking the Lord that it was there, because without it there would have been no work to give us hours of gladness.

Each age, however, is coloured by a collective thought, which is in reality a collective psychological response. This being the case, it would be folly to pretend that the maintaining of detachment in some instances is not a great deal harder than it is in others. During the eighteenth century an appeal to the emotions was bound to be ill-fated; a hundred years later appeals to the reason were in equal disrepute; in our own day it is the appeal to tradition which falls upon deaf ears. If the collective response to all reaction is one of anger and impatience, these emotions are increased when the reactionary has not the excuse of age for his seemingly damnable opinions. By 1802 the tolerant could say that a man who was not a Radical at twenty had no heart, and a man who was a Radical at forty had no head: contemporary feeling flows with the first half of the saying and is neutral to the second. To be a Young Conservative is to throw down a challenge to the times.

Yet, as we have seen, this state of mind is merely a departure; an awakening to conflict which may produce good results, or no results at all. That depends upon the mind. Heidenstam was not content with the Conservative decadence which sufficed for Flandin and Laval, and which brought the Third Republic to its deathbed. He was no politician, but rather a conscientious craftsman. The conflict for him spelt hard work, a synthesis, and at least the hope of reconciliation.

The Young Conservative is lonely—that is his secret and the thorn which bites into his flesh. Fearing those who labour stoutly, and enjoy their pleasures simply, he also envies and admires them. They possess the very attributes he lacks: broad humour, solidarity, a recognition that they live or die together. Wishing to approach them, he can find no point of contact: he is the master, they the hands; and centuries of hard-won battles lie malignantly between them. Sometimes he turns, as Heidenstam did turn, away from both classes, and so towards the nation. Once religion fails, the nation is the one ground on which these two opposing forces may find a common purpose. The nation is not always stronger than the class; but such an instance as the fall of France seems to be the exception to prove the rule or the hard case which never makes good law. It was stronger amongst the German Socialists in 1870, 1914, and in 1933; amongst the British aristocracy in 1939; and amongst the Middle Western farmers in America when Pearl Harbour was attacked. The nation has an equal validity for all the interests of which it is composed: for weal or woe they meet under national flags to-day as in the Middle Ages they met in community around the throne of Peter.

Heidenstam followed the Young Conservative's inevitable progress. From mere decadence—the resignation to *après nous le déluge*—he began to forge some personal equipment. He wrote poems. Bad as they were, their themes did show a measure of advance. He was in love—only with youth, passing pleasures, beauty: but these at least were positive, and less despairing than *le déluge*. The advance quickened to *Thoughts in Loneliness*, a book which bore witness to hard thinking. He had rejected Christianity (even that 'undogmatic Christianity' which was favoured by the Scandinavian Liberals): he longed for work, and discipline, and above all else for contact. The days were gone when he thought of the workers as 'barbaric', or his own class as the chosen guardians of a culture. At last something like a philosophy was taking form in chaos.

It is natural that a writer should hammer out his personal thought largely in terms of literary values, since the world of books becomes the ethos in which he is instinctively at home. Throughout his life there continues a process of acceptance and' rejection, of adverse judgments and of glad responses. Such people are often recognized more truly by their libraries than by their halting conversations. Before his own literary reputation was established, Heidenstam wrote articles and essays on literary subjects; always based upon the thesis that Sweden was capable of greater achievements than she had in fact accomplished. He neither favoured the realists at the expense of the romantics, nor the romantics at the expense of the realists. He maintained instead that the 'grey weather' Scandinavian poetry of the 1880's was an inevitable result of that lush sentiment which had gone before it: each was valuable, yet both were incomplete. He reflected that literary craftsmen were living on their nerves; their nerves were on edge, and they should find a solid value—if it were only resignation. Again, he recognized that Sweden—more than Norway, and a great deal more than Denmark—was a poetic country. As in Britain and in Ireland, lyricists had captured the popular imagination, while writers of stiff prose could never expect to have more than a strictly limited appeal. Fröding, the Vármland poet, was a poet of the people: Selma Lagerlöf, through the untamed beauty of her rhymic prose, had won the hearts of rich and poor, of countrymen, and secretly of urban intellectuals also.

Selma Lagerlöf, Sigrid Undset, and Knut Hamsun knew that they were at war with the ideas of that Liberal Epoch in which they had been born. Not only were their themes outrageous to the Utilitarian mind, but throughout their books there is circumstantial evidence in plenty to prove that they challenged the Victorian age, and held fast their briefs against it. Here Heidenstam was a mere spectator. He was no feminist, yet there is no reason to suppose that he grudged the new emancipation. His puerile conception of two classes, one cultured and the other one 'barbaric', gave place in early life to the knowledge that any class interest as such contained a potential danger to the nation. In the Swedish national past he had found his point of contact. And this, perhaps, is the choice which the Young Conservative mentality must make: for either, retaining every prejudice of birth and education, yet resolved to move with the times at any cost, it becomes cynical and shallow; or else, sublimating these prejudices until they turn to love, it will forget personal discomforts and strive for the betterment of others. This does not mean that the Young Conservative becomes a Young Progressive. He is still a stranger in the modern world; but he has grasped at one permanence, one factor which is neither old nor new—the unfolding history of his people. The more he contemplates the twists and turns of fortune, the stout-hearted resistances and heroic stands, the more conscious he becomes that but for the poor man in his nation, his own family would have been impoverished or extinguished. Heidenstam learnt this sober lesson, and it took him farther still. For he came to see that the heroic qualities, which the Young Conservative admires so much, were in need of cleansing. Even when, in *St. Bridget's Pilgrimage*, he turned from soldiers and statesmen to a national saint, he saw that Bridget's self-will and domineering nature had needed ceaseless contact before they could emerge as Christian charity and zeal. Like Aloysius Gonzaga, Heidenstam, in his own personality, and in what claimed his admiration, was a piece of twisted iron. He was a great writer in so far as he recognized the twist.

He began to find himself, and the literary spirit of his people, and to express them both in short, disjointed verses.

> I've yearned for home now eight long years.
> In my very sleep I have felt the yearning.
> I yearn for home. I yearn where'er I go
> —though not for people ! I long for the soil,
> I yearn for the stones where as a child I played.

And:

> Oh, say not that our elders,
> whose eyes are closed for ever,
> that those we fain would banish
> and from our lives would sever,—

say not their colours vanish
like flowers and like grasses,
that we from hearts efface them
like dust, when one would clear it
from ancient window-glasses.
In power they upraise us,
a host they of the spirit.
The whole white earth enshrouding,
our thoughts too overclouding,
whate'er our fate or fortune,
thoughts that, like swallows crowding,
fly home at evening duly.
A home ! How firm its base is
by walls securely shielded—
our world—the one thing truly
we in this world have builded.[1]

If we read, or preferably speak aloud, *A Lament for Ireland*,
translated by Lady Gregory from Shemus Cartan, we shall
understand how differently this same longing for home, and
for the nation, is expressed by the men of different races:

I do not know of anything under the sky
That is friendly or favourable to the Gael,
But only the sea that our need brings us to,
Or the wind that blows to the harbour
The ship that is bearing us away from Ireland;
And there is reason that these are reconciled with us,
For we increase the sea with our tears,
And the wandering wind with our sighs.

The Swedish fragments and the Irish, both on the themes
of absence from the home and great nostalgia for it, are
wonderfully typical expressions of a racial feeling. While
Heidenstam yearns for the earth and stones on which he
played in childhood, Cartan will not admit to such a simple
longing. As many Irishmen have done, he has grown beyond

[1] All quotations are from *Six Scandinavian Novelists*, by Alrik Gustafson,
with kind permission of the publishers, American-Scandinavian Foundation,
Princeton, U.S.A.

the age when one believes that the old scenes stand still in time, waiting only until the vagrant shall return and be absorbed once more into his native parish. Heidenstam believed that the house-walls were sentinels against all movement in a world outside them: Cartan knew that he was leaving a whole order which, even though he went back to it next year, would have vanished from the waking consciousness for ever. The Swedish simplicity and Irish complexity are two poles upon the planet of nostalgia. No power willed that the Norseman should be absent: but against Cartan's happiness every power of men and devils was continually employed:

> I do not know of anything under the sky
> That is friendly or favourable to the Gael.

While he was forging a personal philosophy of life, and obtaining a balanced outlook upon the literature of Sweden, Heidenstam had expressed himself in verse. Yet, like many lyricists before him, he could voice a final judgment only in the form of prose. *The Tree of the Folkungs* is a novel in the great tradition of the North. Its opening might belong to any of the Sagas—only that it goes farther back in history; to a pre-Christian era:

How the dwarfs lost the horn Mánegarm and how a seed was laid in the earth from which a great tree was to grow, is here to be related. Here we shall tell the story of a race which attained to the highest honour and then was swept away and left no trace behind. What thoughts the mighty ones of this kin had of their golden crowns, when their old age lay before them like cold and slippery stairs descending to hell, and how the unhappy ones lamented their fetters, shall also be told. Let those who will hear these things give heed. Nothing shall be kept back. Vast distances separate them from us, but all human destinies are spun by the same weird sisters.

This, exciting and impersonal, should be contrasted with the first lines of either of Sigrid Undset's medieval novels. They begin in a purposely low key: dates, family-histories, and the relationship between her principal characters and the reigning houses of the day are all established, with a wealth of evidence which the student can check from any textbook. As a Christian apologist, her business is to show that Europe did possess a Christian culture; that the Church's law was held in high esteem; that an absolute virtue was recognized by the scoffer and the sinner, no less than by the pastor and the saint. To do this, she must be accurate and unemotional. But those writers, such as Hamsun and Heidenstam in Scandinavia, who are alive to the importance of all traditions other than the Christian, do not require to prove their case. Proof would be, not only unnecessary, but also disconcerting. In the last analysis, they are *thinking with the blood.*

The Tree of the Folkungs opens with a conflict peculiar to the Swedish spirit—the racial animus between Finn and Scandinavian; would-be conquerors and never-to-be conquered, struggling within a common frontier. It has been written of Sibelius that there is in his nature a substratum of Finnish granite, underlying the elegant Swedish surface; that from his Scandinavian blood he inherits courtesy, affability, the gift of hospitality; and from his Finnish blood independence, self-reliance, a love of solitude, and an unfathomable reserve.[1] These differences are apparent in his music, and Heidenstam (although experiencing them from the Swedish side) does not fail to acknowledge their existence. In *The Tree of the Folkungs* a Finn dwarf, Jorgrimme, is a perpetual menace to the Vikings. Lacking their physical strength and knowledge of the world, he can always outwit them by summoning to his aid the powers of hidden magic.

On the day when a Viking ship returns to unload its plunder by the mound-grave of a shield-maid, Jorgrimme is there, and cries:

"Mound-dwellers! Do you hear? This night the women weep in the hall of Fyrisall. Long is the way thither, seven days' journey.

[1] *Sibelius*, by Cecil Gray (Oxford University Press).

But never before did I hear such wailing. Never before did such
terror fare over the land.

"Strike thy shield hard, mound-maiden ! Rouse thy peers from
the sleep of death ! Now creak the floor-planks behind the stone
of sacrifice in the Sveas' holiest temple. It is Asa Thor's image
that is trembling. Mercy, mercy upon all that has life !"

Then the Viking chieftain lumbers up the mound, taking a
handful of dry earth from his pouch and throwing it down
upon the grave:

"When I set out," he said, "I took this mould from your mound
that it might bring me luck. Generously have you helped me.
Poor was I when I sailed, driven from my father's house, where
too many sons thronged the bench. Homeless I was as the waiting
guillemot under the autumn sky. Since then I have never drained
a horn under sooty roof-tree, nor slept in downy bed, but seven
strongholds I have burnt in Frankland. Now I am rich enough to
buy land for myself, and I am sick and weary of the sea, which my
murmuring crew are so unwilling to leave. The servants of the sea are
thralls of a fickle master. Thralls too are they who writhe in longing
for fame or who see in all their dreams a woman. Therefore
my men are thralls, but I alone am free, for I have no longing
and I love no woman nor anything under the sun. Mound-woman!
—when did so free a man speak with you ? When did so happy
a man stand upon your grave ? Here I offer to you my tokens of
thraldom, my helmet and my sword. The world may go as it will
for me. I shall enjoy my years in peace. Early each morning I
shall go to my trap to fetch what it has caught that night. Then
I shall doze upon my seat of turf in the sunshine and hear corn
growing."

But the dwarf screams back:

"And I tell you that you would do better to go back to your
ship. I tell you chief, I tell you franklin, that if it is peace you
seek, you must fly. For generations without number no man has
beheld such things as are now at hand. The Æsir are now descending upon the land to seek out a seed of vigorous growth, and no
man knows where their choice may fall. . . . From this shoot will

grow a shady tree with tempests and calm stars in its topmost branches. So high will the tree rise that it will overshadow all living things, not only men but the steeds in their stalls and the oxen at the plough, nay, even the wild beasts in the woods. For when its boughs drip sunshine or blood, all will feel it. And all will be hurt when the stem is rent and falls. Thus do the high Æsir speak for me to-night. . . ."

Heidenstam cannot escape the racial conflict. The Viking chief marries one of Jorgrimme's daughters, assuming that she will occupy an inferior position in his household, yet acknowledging that she has some power—whether physical or psychological or quite magical he cannot guess—with which to sway his judgments. This family spreads and grows, as the Æsir prophesied it would do, securing domination, now by firm character, now by brutality, now by peasant cunning. Indeed, they can never rise above the peasant level; subjugating inferiors when they must, they treat them on the whole with a kind of coarse equality: overbearing one day, overfamiliar on the morrow. Neither in youth nor middle age do they find contentment; while they have vitality enough they will wrest honours from the world by violence and yet more prosperity by guile. Quiet settles with the years; coming only to the bowed spirit and the broken flesh.

Here Heidenstam was already toying with the idea of a nature-mysticism which need not exclude Christianity, provided Christianity were recognized as the younger, weaker heir of that antiquity from which both paganism and the Gospel had sprung forth. A teaching Church was quite beyond his vision, and his mind was to harden still more rigidly against it.

How, then, are we to find a place for him in modern letters? Certainly his was always the Young Conservative approach. Faced by the first choice which such an outlook presupposes —the choice between a determination to move with the times at any cost and a deep enquiry into the national past—he made the right selection. But later on, growing away from the notion of superior and inferior classes, he grew into the idea of superior and inferior races. Racial conflict diverted and finally enthralled him. Whereas Sibelius, through the art of music, recognized the useful qualities to be found alike in Finn and Scandinavian, Heidenstam identified the Scandinavians with good qualities, and the Finns with bad ones. Honesty, industry, and thrift belong on one side of the racial border: magic, superstition, double-dealing on the other.

In the downfall of this one writer there is a pretty moral for many politicians. Mix arrogance of race with approbation of society's movement towards its 'pagan roots', and we are left with an 'Ideology', neither pure nor simple. How to rescue love of country, and all that is healthy in the Young Conservative approach, from such a spiritual stagnation is a task which only hard thinking on the part of individuals, and the will to collective sanity, can perform. Heidenstam, sprung from a race which could have taught him better; a good poet, and one whose mind was fertilized continually by beauty, did not keep himself untarnished. There comes the warning; from an unlikely place, that it may be pondered the more deeply.

KNUT HAMSUN

JOHN GALSWORTHY, when he was young enough to be repelled by the light manner of people who were facing heavy tasks, and therefore not yet fascinated by their skilful evasions, their conscious and semi-conscious mendacity, and all that a cynical age has come to associate with the processes of governmental thought, described, in his book *The Freelands*, a typical house-party at which typical 'bigwigs' were assembled. These august gentlemen presented certain problems to their hostess. She must not, for instance, allow a financial expert to monopolize the evening; but she must make sure that the Irish and Indian Questions were ventilated by men who had climbed to power upon them, and that the Land Question had a half-hour after dinner to itself. It was an excellent digestive. While it would not send the company to sleep, it would not challenge the cold salmon to a duel or the roast pheasant to a tourney.

Galsworthy understood his world—the British upper class during a period of transition. But he did not understand the land, any more than they did. Had he done so, he would never have allowed it to be treated as a question. Instead, he would have seen it as an answer: an answer to the 'why?' of life; yet first, and pre-eminently to the 'how?' A good farmer has advanced a long way in the art of living; for his is one of the rarer occupations which teaches philosophy without textbooks and mystical theology without set meditations. Everything pertaining to life is encountered, if not on the farmer's daily round, at least in the yearly cycle on his holding. He is therefore better equipped to give advice than to receive it. But this has the tragic-comical result that an awareness of all human limitations prevents his speaking boldly, while those who are less aware mind his business for him.

In these unpromising conditions; of a few dumb men who know and many babblers who know not, our surprise runs a dead heat with our gladness when we do receive an answer.

It is always accidental. Mary Webb begins a diary to pass
the winter evenings by her cottage fireside; Llewelyn Powys
is attacked by a regiment of tubercular bacilli; Selma Lagerlöf
is devoured by homesickness for her girlhood days in Vármland; A. G. Street amuses his family by scribbling a few lines
on the blank pages of a milk-book. These men and women,
although possessing a fund of first-hand knowledge, of heavy
humour and light wit, of sympathy and patience, no more set
out to be professional writers than a young man sets out to be
bread-winner and father when he kisses a girl amidst the drunken
beauty of midsummer. Midsummer madness forces the youth,
he knows not whither: a mad desire to pass away the evening
lays hold of an occasional farmer, or his daughter, or his wife,
and before they know it, they are country writers.

In human society there are rifts enough without encouraging
and broadening a fresh one, between countrymen and towns-
men. We should not grant experience to the one, and deny
it wholly to the other. Yet the experience differs; its quality
is not the same. The clerkly type, holding more than pride of
place in modern letters, has written freely, even of the country.
Arnold Bennett thought—and made his readers think—that the
industrial landscape possessed a rugged charm; and his song
was echoed by more than one poet of the 1930's. Housman
created an imaginary Shropshire, just as Theodore Powys
created an imaginary Dorset. Their influence made sure that
village inns, and barns, and haystacks, should be rediscovered
by those who sought the Simple Life from Saturday to Monday
in the month of August. Not all their writing was untruthful,
nor was all their love of simplicity a pose. They gave to the
town worker what was, for a time at least, his manifest desire:
a vision which turned the Green Line bus into a prairie-wagon
and the Hind's Head at Bray, or the Spread Eagle at Midhurst,
into a country tavern. Love is a transforming power. Under
its eternal absolution sows' ears do become silk purses.

Through the 1920's and the 1930's this second-hand experience of the country was sufficient for town-workers: their
work lay in one direction and their pleasure, mostly vicarious,

in another. But when Britain found herself at war and Eire
imprisoned by her 'coastline; with foreign cargoes measured
against the lives of ships and sailors, the townsman looked
to the countryman for food. Now he would not be happy
to contemplate a Shropshire in which all the lads were hanged
or a Dorset where all the maidens drowned themselves.
Questions of the day were rather more realistic: What of·the
oat crops high up on the Wrekin? And: Were the Dorset
Horn ewes still lambing twice a year? Furthermore, the
townsman on holiday no longer slept in barns. After twelve
hours of pitching corn, he was glad to undress in a room whose
walls were gay with excerpts from St. John and Revelation;
to wash in a cracked basin, and to lie down upon luxurious
feather-bedding. This was not perhaps 'The Life'; but it
was a man's job, and a woman's too.

As first-hand experience of the country has filtered through
to the urban populations of more than one nation since the
war broke out, so has the demand for books whose facts and
figures can be checked. While humility has increased, pride
has been rekindled. The man who pitched corn in August or
split tree-roots in December knows how these operations
should be managed. Under the stress of this new judgment,
serious country writing is demanded. The pattern of all such
books can be found in Scandinavia; for Hamsun's *Growth of
the Soil* has not anywhere been rivalled since its publication
a quarter-century ago.

Authorship achieves universal acceptance and respect, not
only when it produces a great book, but also when that book
is outstanding in its class, and therefore a type destined for
many imitations. Flaubert's *Madame Bovary* and Jacobsen's
Neils Lyhne were patterns for decadent writing in the future;
Dostoevski's *The Idiot* showed once and for all how the science
of psychology could serve the art of fiction; *All Quiet on the
Western Front*, in a lesser sphere, taught every ex-soldier with
a literary bent how to make the most of war experience.
Like Flaubert, Dostoevski, and Remarque, Hamsun carved
out a mould, and invented a special style to suit it.

The finished product owes its existence to three distinct philosophies—realism, a return to the primitive, and the conception of farming as a satisfying religion. In English literature we can find parallels for the first and second; the third as yet has not advanced beyond Germany and Scandinavia. Hardy, Galsworthy, and Wells, together with their thousands of disciples, are realists in the sense that they regard good writing and accurate photography under the same judgment. They think that a writer should portray, with a maximum of self-effacement, the real world in which he lives: we must be able to check his places from the atlas, his times from the calendar or *Bradshaw*, and his people from men and women with whom we are otherwise acquainted. D. H. Lawrence, who preached a return to the primitive outspokenly in essays and implicitly in novels, only carried such realism on to another level: his are ordinary characters whose natural impulses unchecked land them in unlikely and sometimes morally disastrous situations.

Hamsun was not influenced directly by the English Realists. He had many examples nearer home, and his own struggles against a society which did not seem to want him furnished good material for photographs of physical and mental anguish. His first book, *Hunger*, was written by a man actually starving in a garret. The parallel between Hamsun and Galsworthy or Wells in that which concerns one part of his philosophy, and with D. H. Lawrence in what concerns another, is useful because it shows that the third and most important part— farming conceived as a satisfying religion—has never been taught in English letters. On the other hand, it has been taught in Prussia. Its exponents there have been, not only such first-class novelists as Weichert, but it has appeared in *Secret Sentence*, by Vicki Baum—a work of entertainment. Weichert framed it in a verse:

Wir brauchen keinen Besitz.	We don't want chattels
Wir brauchen Arbeit, Armut	Rather do we crave
und ein bisschen Zeit.	For work and poverty
	And time to make our souls.

In *Secret Sentence* Vicki Baum allows no peace to Joachim Burthe until he has learnt to obey the laws of nature by working as a primary producer, with his hands. Every other occupation —retailing, politics, or business—appear to these writers in the form of waste and damage: they are wasteful of the community's resources and damaging to the individual spirit. Because there is no parallel in English letters, it is difficult to separate this religion of toil from that return to the primitive which we associate with D. H. Lawrence. Yet it must be done. The philosophical side of the new political ideology in Europe springs from a double source. Some National Socialists, for instance, believed that their country would perish unless they forgot all Christian virtues; being absolutely free, from outward restraint and inner conscience, to lust and rob and kill. That is Lawrence's return to the primitive, carried to its logical conclusion. Such a philosophy is anti-Christian and anti-cultural, of course; but it is also anti-intellectual. The human brain is no longer the centre of decision. Others were not attracted by this myth. They felt that the economic side of life had become complicated to a degree which prevented men from being enriched by natural wisdom. Their desire was not for a return to the primitive, but for a return to days before the Industrial Revolution. Land-owners then were wise because the land had made them so: land-workers were happy because their labour was so satisfying that they required to ask no questions. The Prussian State and the Prussian way of life were both founded to a great extent on this set of values. When such values were menaced by Germany's entrance into industrial competition, they were reflected from outside— from nowhere so much as Scandinavia, in no work so much as Hamsun's.

The normal man's reaction to this type of thinking is to say: Civilization has been built up inch by inch, with blood and tears and sweat. Our hold on progress is precarious. If once we look backwards, we shall lose a part at least of the ground which has been won so hardly. The faster we progress from here, the more likely it is that mistakes will be corrected.

This is sound and healthy. It is endorsed by the Catholic
Church; for the great encyclicals accept economics at the
point which they have reached, insisting only that no section
of the community shall be liquidated in order to hasten the
advancement of the others. Hamsun is not a Catholic. In
any case he feels himself the champion of a section which *is*
being liquidated; and he is therefore incapable of the popes'
more balanced judgment. He sees a world whose natural
resources are being exploited to produce wealth which is only
real on paper; a world where cunning can triumph over skill,
superficial sentiment over ingrained loyalty, and passing
fashions over the cultural habits of races, families, and nations.

Although he is in a minority, which is almost a minority of
one, he is neither moralist, preacher, nor crank. He regards life
with interest and humour. No creature, whether calf, foal,
or human baby is too small to arouse his powers of penetration:
no substance—not even a potato—is too humble for a lyric:

What was that about potatoes? Were they just a thing from
foreign parts, like coffee; a luxury, an extra? Oh, the potato is
a lordly fruit; drought or downpour, it grows and grows all the
same. It laughs at the weather, and will stand anything; only
deal kindly with it, and it yields fifteenfold again. Not the blood
of a grape, but the flesh of a chestnut, to be boiled or roasted,
used in every way. A man may lack corn to make bread, but give
him potatoes and he will not starve. Roast them in embers, and
there is supper; boil them in water, and there's a breakfast ready.
As for meat, it's little is needed beside. Potatoes can be served
with what you please; a dish of milk, a herring is enough. The rich
eat them with butter; poor folk manage with a tiny pinch of salt. . . .

Wells and Lawrence created styles through which their very
different philosophies of life could be unfolded. Wells's style
—always wordy, often laboured and unreal—would make us
think that the fate of *Homo Sapiens* depends on the measurable
amount of knowledge which each separate man is able and
willing to acquire: Lawrence's—sensual, drowsy, and incon-
sequential—would compel us to reject the intellect, and to

feel the passions of men, the moods of landscape, and the caprice of a morally neutral destiny behind them. Hamsun also teaches through a style; although it is impossible to tell whether he created it to serve his ends, or whether it grew in a natural way out of his material. To gauge its quality, one should read that most strange of openings—that abrupt encounter with a landscape and a lone mortal up against it:

The long, long road over the moors and up into the forest—who trod it into being first of all? Man, a human being, the first that came here. There was no path before he came. Afterward, some beast or other, following the faint tracks over marsh and moorland, wearing them deeper; after these again some Lapp gained scent of the path, and took that way from fjeld to fjeld, looking to his reindeer. Thus was made the road through the great Almenning—the common tracts without an owner; no-man's-land.

The man comes, walking toward the north. He bears a sack, the first sack, carrying food and some few implements. A strong, coarse fellow, with a red iron beard, and little scars on face and hands; sites of old wounds—were they gained in toil or fight? Maybe the man has been in prison, and is looking for a place to hide; or a philosopher, maybe, in search of peace. This or that, he comes; the figure of a man in this great solitude. He trudges on; bird and beast are silent all about him; now and again he mutters a word or two, speaking to himself. "Eyah—well, well . . ." so he speaks to himself. Here and there, where the moors give place to a kindlier spot, an open space in the midst of the forest; he lays down the sack and goes exploring; after a while he returns, heaves the sack on his shoulders again, and trudges on. So through the day, noting time by the sun; night falls, and he throws himself down on the heather, resting on his arms.

After several days he explores a site more carefully, and then:

The worst of his task had been to find the place; this no-man's place, but his. Now, there was work to fill his days. He started at once, stripping birch bark in the woods farther off, while the

sap was still in the trees. The bark he pressed and dried, and when
he had gathered a heavy load, carried it all the miles back to the
village to be sold for building. Then back to the hillside, with new
sacks of food and implements; flour and pork, a cooking-pan,
a spade—out and back along the way he had come, carrying loads
all the time. A born carrier of loads, a lumbering barge of a man
in the forest—oh, as if he loved his calling, tramping long roads
and carrying heavy burdens; as if life without a load upon one's
shoulders were a miserable thing, no life for him.

One day he came up with more than the load he bore; came
leading three goats in a leash. He was proud of his goats as if they
had been horned cattle, and tended them kindly. Then came
the first stranger passing, a nomad Lapp; at sight of the goats he
knew that this was a man who had come to stay, and spoke to
him.

"You going to live here for good?"

"Ay," said the man.

"What's your name?"

"Isak. You don't know of a woman body anywhere'd come and
help?"

"No. But I'll say a word of it to all I meet."

"Ay, do that. Say I've creatures here, and none to look to
them." . . .

So Hamsun's style unfolds itself throughout these early
pages: the lack of setting, the conception of toil as a necessity
for man's physical and moral health; the terse dialogue, so
natural that there is an illusion of reading the original.
Presently the woman comes. Her name is Inger. They marry;
the farm begins to grow:

Inger was a blessing too, in other ways. No clever head, not
great in wit maybe—but she had two lambing ewes with some of
her kinsfolk, and brought them down. It was the best they could
have wished for at the hut; sheep with wool and lambs, four new
head to their stock about the place; it was growing, getting bigger;
a wonder and a marvel how their stock was grown. . . .

A time comes when the State takes notice of Isak, insisting
that he shall buy his land and name it. Two different sheriffs

are concerned in drawing up the deeds; and Hamsun enjoys
himself at the expense of pompous writing.

Sheriff Heyerdahl drew up his report in elegant phrasing. Sheriff
Geisler had written: "The man will also have to pay land tax every
year; he cannot afford to pay more for the place than fifty *Daler*,
in annual instalments over ten years. The State can accept his
offer, or take away his land and the fruits of his work." Heyerdahl
wrote: "He now humbly begs to submit this application to the
Department: that he be allowed to retain his land, upon which,
albeit without right of possession, he has up to this present effected
considerable improvements, for a purchase price of fifty *Speciedaler*,
the amount to be paid in annual instalments as may seem fit to the
Department to appropriate the same." . . .

Geisler, who settled every question out of hand, named the
place 'Sellanraa'. It is Sellanraa Farm, a barren waste until
Isak's lifelong toil transformed it into a prosperous holding,
which retains a character more clearly defined than those of
human beings. The humans are judged by their reactions to
the farm; Isak serves it well, and he is therefore good; his
son Eleseus has always a divided loyalty, seeking quick success
from many ventures, and we are made to share in Hamsun's
condemnation of him. After a spell away from work,

Eleseus was somehow changed; whatever it might be, something
in him had been warped, and quietly spoiled; he was not bad, but
something blemished. Had he lacked a guiding hand those last few
years? What could his mother do to help him now? Only stand
by him, and agree. She could let herself be dazzled by her son's
bright prospects for the future, and stand between him and his
father, to take his part—she could do that. . . .

His prospects are always bright; and yet they lead him
nowhere. On the farm he talks boldly about his adventures
in the city, while the family admire him and laugh at him, in
turns, for his black suit, stiff collar, and umbrella; once in
the city, he cannot command high wages, so that he is forced
to gamble, and finally to write home for a remittance. Sigrid

Undset, valuing all men upon a Christian basis, would have given him some redeeming feature: to Hamsun he is a waste product, a wasted life; an unproductive unit in society. Such a gospel of production belongs to the nineteenth century rather than to the modern way of thinking; and it is one of many resemblances between Hamsun and Carlyle. Both are Puritans, but neither is especially a Christian; both hold that every man succeeds by his own efforts, yet that some are given a power which will sustain them, while the power is withheld, capriciously, from others. Isak had it: Eleseus lacked it; one was predestined to salvation, and the other to damnation.

The Victorian world, which had not experienced unemployment, frustrated zeal in war and peace, and a revolt in favour of disorder, could preach the blessings of toil to a believing public. The twentieth century is embittered by the knowledge that there is a nigger in the woodpile. We do not know what the nigger is: some say faith; some, loss of faith; some, economics; some, the social system; some, the bankers, the politicians, the rich, the poor, the Russians, the Germans, or the Jews. There is agreement on one point alone—that man's best intentions, and his hardest efforts, are frustrated. Hamsun was insufficiently a modern product to hold this view as part of his ordinary equipment; but he knew that it was held by others, so he created a nigger to satisfy their craving. This was the town. The town was incalculably evil; it produced only to destroy; it made bad characters, and spoilt good ones. Furthermore, it plundered the country, triumphing over simple men by cunning, and prostituting rural wisdom into urban guile.

It cannot be judged how far this was a real belief, and how far Hamsun adopted it to satisfy his public. He gave them the two things which the feeling of our century desires: a nigger and a way to beat him. This way was, of course, hard work —loyalty to Sellanraa Farm. Yet Hamsun revolted consciously against the liberal philosophy under whose sway he had been born. When he was a young man liberal society had been content to see him starve, and it was so well satisfied with its own achievements that *Hunger*, an attack on liberalism, was sponsored by the leading progressives of the day. Such a gesture was not lost on Hamsun, for he could understand the contempt behind it. These literary men were not serious people: they wanted an unusual book; a sensational book which would only show the true strength of their position.

Reduced to its bones, his indictment of progressives could be framed as follows: You make a song and dance about the poor, but you take care not to meet them, and you wouldn't like them if you did. You say that your object is to uplift them. Uplift them to what? Your own level? Then they must learn the art of commanding a week's wage without doing a week's work; of producing nothing with their hands, and of birth-control, which is the murder of children and the destruction of the race. You will give them a smattering of culture, which is not real culture in any case; and from them you will take their loyalty to families and homes; their broad humour, because you are too prudish to enjoy it, and their zest for life, because you yourselves are zestless. You will spoon-feed humanity until man can do nothing for himself; the earth will lose its people; and then, perhaps, you will be contented. I hate you, and I am going to fight you. Very few will listen to what I have to say. That doesn't matter in the least. I know where my duty lies, and I have the sense to do it.

He did it. Mostly by allowing the progressives full rein to voice the thoughts within them. Here, for instance, is Fru Heyerdahl, pleading in court for a girl who has slain her new-born child:

"We, women," said Fru Heyerdahl, "are an unfortunate and oppressed moiety of humanity. It is the men who make the laws, and we women have not a word to say in the matter. But can any man put himself in the position of a woman in childbirth? Has he ever felt the dread of it, ever felt the terrible pangs, ever cried aloud in the anguish of that hour? In the present instance, it is a serving-girl who has borne the child. A girl unmarried, and consequently trying all through the critical time to hide her condition. And why must she seek to hide it? Because of society. Society despises the unmarried woman who bears a child. Not only does society offer her no protection, but it persecutes her, pursues her with contempt and disgrace. Atrocious! No human creature with any heart at all could help feeling indignant at such a state of things. Not only is the girl to bring a child into the world, a thing in itself surely hard enough, but she is to be treated as a criminal for that very fact. . . . Think, consider what she has been through during all the period of pregnancy, what suffering she has endured in striving to hide her condition, and all the time never knowing where to turn for herself and the child when it comes. . . . The child is at least killed in kindness."

This girl's name is Barbro. She has nothing to do with Isak and Inger, the main people in the book; but Hamsun draws her character at length to show how a fickle girl can retard man's progress in his fight with nature on the land. After a time in Bergen, where she was wanted for child-murder by the police, she settled with a man named Axel on his holding. Axel wanted to marry her; but she would not be tied, and it is for the murder of his baby that she is now answering in court. Fru Heyerdahl's eloquence gains her an acquittal; and afterwards this busy woman takes Barbro into service. Immediately Barbro goes back to her old ways; she has been so greatly corrupted by the town that she must have admiration, and will prostitute herself to gain it. Fru Heyerdahl finds her out, and heaps her with reproaches:

"After I've saved you from the clutches of the Law. . . ."
"As for that," answers Barbro, "I'd have been just as pleased if you hadn't."
"And that's all the thanks I get," says her mistress.
"Least said the better, perhaps," says Barbro. "I wouldn't have got more than a month or two, anyway, and done with it."

Fru Heyerdahl is speechless for a moment; ay, for a little she stands saying nothing; only opening and closing her mouth. The first thing she says is to tell the girl to go; she will have no more of her.

"Just as you please," says Barbro. . . .

Hamsun's belief is that some people are born low. This
lowness has nothing to do with social class, with poverty or
wealth; although it may be due to occupation. He considers
it unlikely that a merchant or domestic servant will possess
the major virtues. The whole question comes back to varying
doses of original sin; one character is born with a large dose,
and another with a small one. Yet even Inger did not survive
a visit to the town; she returned to Sellanraa filled with large
ideas, too proud to work beside her husband, and generally
neglectful of her duties. Slowly the farm brings its influence
to bear, forcing her to acknowledge single-minded love,
absolute service, undivided loyalty. When dealing with Inger,
Hamsun shows himself tolerant of carnal lapses. Men and
women do not demonstrate love after the flesh alone, but
by the general course on which their hearts and minds are set.
When Inger has been unfaithful, it is in this way that she and
Isak wrestle with their problem:

> One night she lifted up on her elbow and said:
> "Isak?"
> "What is it?" says Isak.
> "Are you awake?"
> "Ay."
> "Nay, 'twas nothing," says Inger. "But I've not been as I ought."
> "What?" says Isak.
> Ay, so much he said, and rose up on his elbow in turn.
> They lay there, and went on talking. Inger is a matchless
> woman after all; and with a full heart.
> "I've not been as I ought towards you, and I'm sorry about it."
> The simple words move him; this barge of a man is touched,
> ay, he wants to comfort her, knowing nothing of what is the matter,
> but only that there is none like her.
> "Naught to cry about, my dear," says Isak. "There's none of
> us can be as we ought."
> "Nay, 'tis true," she answers gratefully.
> Ay, Isak had a strong, sound way of taking things; straightened
> them out, he did, when they went crooked. "None of us can be as
> we ought." Ay, he was right. The god of the heart—for all
> that he is a god, he goes a deal of crooked ways, goes out

adventuring, the wild thing that he is, and we can see it in his
looks. One day rolling in a bed of roses and licking his lips
and remembering things; next day with a thorn in his foot,
desperately trying to get it out. Die of it? Never a bit, he's as
well as ever. A nice look out it would be if he were to die.
And Inger's trouble passed off too; she got over it; but she keeps
on with her hours of devotion, and finds a merciful refuge there.
Hard-working and patient and good she is now every day,
knowing Isak different from all other men, and wanting none
but him.

Through these characters, their strivings, mistakes, the
constant renewal of grace within them, and above all through
the farm, which is their life and reason for being alive itself,
Hamsun gives his message. It is sometimes repugnant to the
Christian approach; it is still more polaric to the highly-
cultured outlook of our times. But with the former it has
points of intersection. As the early Christians saw their own
Gospel as a 'Way', for Hamsun also toil, simplicity, and
service are hills which men must scale if they would attain to
serenity, their haven. Much of that which he says of the
land's neglect, the ruthlessness of capital, and yet of ownership
as ordained by God, has been stated in the letters of Pope
Leo and Pope Pius. The constructive lives on, while only
the destructive is so much waste material. Thus Hamsun's
other books, dwelling upon such characters as Barbro and
Eleseus, and drawing no counterparts to Isak, have very justly
perished.

During Norway's invasion and subjugation, Hamsun became
associated with the victors. It is understandable at the present
time that Norwegians should not be able to assess his work
without seeing a traitor's hand behind it. One can only plead
once more that a judgment of art must be suspended until
time has separated the creation from a creator who has been,
however rightfully, condemned. In all European countries
there is a body of opinion, neither Liberal (in the sense of
anti-clerical and urban) on the one hand, nor Fascist on the
other. But for an evil choice, Hamsun might have led the

peasant farmers of a regenerated Norway. It is perhaps the task of those who read his books to measure how far the teaching they contain is against all human progress, and how far it merely recognizes limitations, takes warning from mistakes, so rendering a real advance more easy than it would otherwise have been. No resolve could be more salutary at the present time than this: to be flexible in our approach to learning; to condemn nothing until it cries out for condemnation; looking for the best in all things, to remember that love itself is a work of art, and so a work of healing.

THE INFLUENCE OF MUSIC

GRIEG AND SIBELIUS

SHAW, in his *Quintessence of Ibsenism,* forced a conflict between those who accepted and those who rejected the nineteenth-century Idea in Scandinavian letters. It was a barren conflict, and the time has come when we should leave it. Jonas Lie, a contemporary and compatriot of Ibsen, held that craftsmen should remain aloof from what are called 'questions of the day'. Knowing how fatally writing has degenerated into pamphleteering (have we not our book-clubs of the Right, of the Left, and of Religion ?), few would doubt that his was a salutary warning. There is a possible neutrality for the craftsman and the artist; although, like neutrality for nations, it is as precarious as it is highly valued. And, in the way that some nations are more blest in this respect by geography and ethnography than others, so some arts can hold aloof, without reproachings or encroachings.

Such a privileged position has been granted to the art of the ear; to music, its composition and its playing. Nor has the privilege stopped short at mere immunity from conflict. When the conflict has died down, even sometimes when it has been fiercest, both combatants have learnt from music, each one resting his case upon her judgment. What a sanity this is ! It is as though, after a great war, victor and vanquished were to choose some little state and to tell her frankly: "Our wells of truth are poisoned from long practice in the art of lying. You had no need to lie. Now tell us the truth, and we in humility will listen !"

The little nation of our choice, although outside the conflict, was not for an instant outside the brotherhood of man, nor was she divorced from the Fatherhood of God; in the same way music, while refusing to join the other arts in their championing of human causes, was still an art of humans.

To think of her otherwise, to put her on a pinnacle, or confine her in a prison, would be the height of folly. All five senses are bridges along which impressions travel to the soul; now, through seeing, a lovely picture or a splendid truth; now, through touching, a fine texture; through scenting, a spring morning or an autumnal dusk; through tasting, the bread of earth, and the Bread of Heaven; through hearing, music—music which is so unfettered that she can paint in sound.

If the senses are bridges, each one carrying an army of impressions to the soul, the soul itself sends out, from its own substance, guides and pilots to carry those impressions home. There is a joyous riot of meeting. We hear bird-song, we behold the sunrise, and we smell the earth—for us all three of these impressions, and many more besides, convey the idea of early morning. And, if it is futile and pedantic to separate them from each other, so, too, it is futile and pedantic to say that writing has one function and music has another. Two books, although of equal greatness, may be so unalike that we feel they belong to different arts; one book and one piece of music may be so similar in spirit that we know writer and composer to have been using identical material. The same is true of painting: Raphael, moved by outline, and Titian, moved by flecks of light, were working through vastly different media; Goya, making his faces 'sing', and Debussy, composing wordless songs, were working through the same.

To arrive at understanding of a foreign people, where facts, however accurate and careful, remain helpless until they are fired by intuition, those who would understand must beware of shutting each scrap of knowledge, and each fragment of experience, into different cells. At school there was, in this way, an hour for history and an hour for the study of a language; so much ill-spared time with the teacher of music, and so much more—perhaps one day a week—with the teacher of modelling or drawing. A segregation of aspects may be necessary for order: it is the death of flair. Let the man who disagrees count up the people whom he knows to have left school, their hearts on fire with the love of learning; he will

find the fingers of one hand sufficient for the task. Then let him contrast with this puny number that overwhelming number who, in face of every setback, are in love with their professions.

The yeoman farmer is an excellent example. Believing that farming is an art, he will travel hundreds of miles to study the masterpieces of his fellow artists: believing it a science, he will watch over each advance in agricultural technics: believing that history can guide him through the managerial problems of his holding, he will spend hours in the company of garrulous old men; listening while they recall the crop-rotations of two or four score years ago. This willingness to adventure out of grooves, this recognition that men learn a few things precisely, yet a great many more by intuition, is necessary for the love of a profession: it is imperative for the understanding of a foreign people.

Following the Shavian method, we could form a mind's-eye picture of the Scandinavian background; and against it we could see trackless forests, icebound fjords, and ancient manors built upon headlands in the sea. With pertinacity we might even discern the figure of a man. This man would be a type: the type of a race which accepted Christianity only to reject the Holy Roman Empire. We should note his skill as a hunter and his prowess as a sailor; his solitude; his deep religious conscience. But then, when these characteristics obtruded themselves into the Liberal Epoch, so that Shaw was forced to explain away such dramas as *The Master Builder*, *The Wild Duck*, and *Little Eyolf* with the use of many clichés, we should grow perplexed. Perplexity, at just this point, has always frustrated students of Scandinavian letters. To them it is suggested that there was a different conflict, in the nineteenth century itself, between Northern writers and Northern musical composers.

We have here to be very careful with our terms. If music is in truth an arbiter, she does not fight. Nor does a mother fight when she must decide some issue which has cleft her menfolk. A wise mother does not even decide outright between them: she suggests, she raises the dispute to a higher level;

she says that the dispute belongs only to a given hour, and that there are less transitory questions. The result of arbitration was, in this case, to lessen enmity between the menfolk, and to precipitate interior conflict: now, instead of each son's wanting the same thing (perhaps an heirloom, perhaps a personal favour) each desired to be less greedy, and so to please the mother. Music is a successful arbiter, but music does precipitate interior conflict. When, after the Reformation, members of the new Church in England listened to Byrd's Masses, they had no fear that they were being subjected to Catholic propaganda; and yet how acutely they must have felt that Byrd's music criticized their stubborn rejection of the past, and their harsh treatment of the Catholics. We can imagine, too, how some men, in favour of dictatorship, are disquieted by Beethoven's trumpet-calls to freedom.

Music fulfilled this same task during the Liberal Epoch in Scandinavia: there was no enmity between Ibsen the writer and Grieg the musical composer; there was rather a partnership, during the course of which letters were criticized and lifted up by music. If Grieg had lived at another time or place, Ibsen's work would have been a materialist's comment on a materialistic age; he might have left us *Ghosts* and *A Doll's House*, but he would not have been inspired to write *Peer Gynt* or *The Master Builder*. These are his greatest works because they are the most intuitive—that is, spiritual—and traditional —that is, Scandinavian. It is here that Grieg enlarges the art of the ear until it functions as an art of the eye; and to do this he uses Ibsen as his medium.

Grieg, living from 1843 to 1907, was a contemporary of the Liberal Writers. He shared with Ibsen the tonic of Scottish blood; his grandfather had fled to Norway after fighting at Culloden, and his father, at Bergen, held the post of British Consul; also with Ibsen, he shared the joy of witnessing Norwegian independence. His mother, on the other hand, was peasant—or, more accurately, yeoman—and it was she who taught him music. At the Leipzig Conservatorium he fell so deeply under the influence of Mendelssohn and Schumann that for a long time he believed one of Germany's missions was to be music-master to the world. A quarter of a century later Sibelius's teachers were to fill him with the same nonsense, and he, too, was to rebel against it. Because in the eighteen sixties Germany had developed, not only a musical technique, but also what may be called a 'philosophy of music', Grieg's rebellion was delayed. Returning as far north as Copenhagen, he endeavoured to apply this musical philosophy at home. If the German songs and dances required special *dramatis personae*, Scandinavia must provide them also: thick-headed louts, innocent young maidens; shoemakers, charcoal-burners, witches; and the whole Black Forest motley. Scandinavia had got what it expected, but not what it desired. Grieg, forcing his talent on to the German last, was pinched, and therefore most unhappy. He was so unhappy that, in the middle of an age which laughed at everything either old or native, he turned to an ancient peasant for advice. The peasant was Richard Nordrák; a man who composed and played for his own amusement, caring little for the good opinion of foreigners, and troubling still less to mince his words. The advice which Nordrák gave to Grieg can be summarized as follows: "Our people are hard, and strong, and simple. They have never imagined Christianity without the cross, and they never will imagine bread—or for that matter, culture—which has not been won by sweat. Purge all this elfery from your system! Then stay up North; put your ear to the ground; still better, to the keyhole of the nearest cottage: in time you stand a chance of doing something for Norwegian music. . . ."

As this study grows, it will help if we find a parallel to sustain us in our progress. What better than that of the Irish 'Middle Nation'? It can be measured, not only against the fact of a people's return to its national source, but also against the actual return of actual craftsmen. The advice which Grieg heard from Richard Nordrák was in all essentials the same sermon which any Irish peasant would have preached to writers of the 'Middle Nation'. As Grieg abandoned the artificial music of Leipzig, going north to hear what he could hear, so Synge abandoned the great houses of the Pale to discover how much living art had been preserved amongst the tinkers, penny minstrels, and innkeepers' daughters of the West. Both ventured a great deal: both were amply rewarded. In Gaelic Ireland Synge discovered the old stories, and he hammered out a new form through which they could be made attractive and intelligible to his English-speaking hearers; in Norwegian Norway Grieg discovered the old tunes, and was inspired to give *them* a form which would make them beloved of every musically educated European. And, as in Ireland the native country was always 'just around the corner'—one bumped into it at market, a few yards on the far side of the park gates, and of course in the Catholic 'chapel'—Norwegian Norway was scarcely an inch beneath the cosmopolitan veneer of Christiania, or the Swedish 'court circles', or the stilted Dano-Norse of the Reformation Bible.

Such men who go exploring, whether for letters or for music, become filled with missionary zeal; the more they are victimized by their own class, and misunderstood while living by the world in general, the more certain they grow that a good case cannot be overstated. Synge proceeded from *The Tinker's Wedding* to the *Playboy*, and from there to *Deirdre of the Sorrows* ; and the farther he went, leaving a witty mood for a world of pathos, the more triumphantly was his case established. The same certainty—the sure knowledge that he was performing an essential task—goaded Grieg from fair success to super-excellence. Also it afforded him protection. Without a stubborn will no craftsman can hope to stay the course: his friends deluge him with sweet reason; his enemies invite him to 'curse God and die'; the broad-bottomed mass of public opinion is blissfully unaware of his existence.

Of course if he, the craftsman, does leave even a few stragglers behind, staying in the race for any time at all, he is bound to receive an odd cheer from some old rider, who is firmly in the saddle. This was Grieg's good fortune when he went to Rome, taking his piano concerto, and presenting it fearfully to Liszt. Liszt, his head filled with dolorous Hungarian

noises, must have wondered whence came this exquisite lyrical feeling, this limpidity of sound, and the stern, uncouth young man who could produce them. A lesser personage would have said that the concerto was not down his street: Liszt played it at sight, praised it, maintained that such work had a future, and sent Grieg home rejoicing. Grieg was always lucky with his opposites: perhaps in a leisured age each man has time to look beyond his street; perhaps these days we have no great art, so that what passes for art is bounded by some frontiers; perhaps Grieg himself was tactful. Having wrested encouragement from Liszt, he worked the more spectacular miracle of gaining sympathy from Ibsen. The point deserves some labour. A musician whose self-imposed task was to revive Norwegian music gained the sympathy of a writer whose acknowledged vocation was to debunk Norwegian morals, traditions, and beliefs.

Nor did the miracle end at the establishment of sympathy between them. Ibsen listened, then he co-operated, then, finally, he learnt. He learnt in the first place that the social drama would remain unattractive—that it would in fact be lifeless—unless it contained some characters and situations sufficiently bold and unusual to capture the imagination. For Ibsen was tempted—and this he must have known—to believe that liberal ideas had significance outside the nineteenth century and outside northern Europe. A writer must admit the validity of all times, or he will admit the validity of none. But for Grieg's adventurings into the Norwegian past, Ibsen would have worked from the assumption that Norway's history began in 1840, that its middle class was of overwhelming interest, and that its transitory social problems were world-wide.

Grieg's influence was manifested chiefly through *The Master Builder*. Here, in the character of Solnes we have Ibsen's nearest approach to a universal figure; here, in the setting of the play, we are allowed to escape from something so limited as a bourgeois drawing-room to something so transcendental as a tower. For, if Solnes was not a saint, and thus a phenomenon which crops up here, there, everywhere, and at every time, he had at least the possibilities of sainthood. He was a little mad: mad enough to be in love with the idea of building high, and mad enough to risk his neck on a last, almighty gamble. We accept him, mad as he is, not because we were reared upon the social drama, but because we were reared on stories of the saints. If St. Simon could live for years upon a pillar, we see no reason why Solnes should not have wished to grow giddy on a tower; if St. Francis could not bear a world in which he was afraid of kissing lepers, we can understand why Solnes could not bear a world in which he was consumed by the dread of falling. We venerate the saints because their madness was successful; we can at least be sorry for the Master Builder when *his* madness failed. We are not sorry for Nora—not at all. We grant that she was no less sane than we are; no less calculating; and therefore doomed to the disappointments which we ourselves experience. Had Ibsen given to the world nothing more exciting than a collection of frustrated wives, he would have lived and died obscure. Because he gave us one figure, eccentric to the point of universality, he is universally accepted. This last-minute change of mediocrity to greatness Ibsen owed to Grieg: yet more deeply, he owed it to music, the gentle arbiter which gives rise to fierce interior conflict. Beyond Grieg music went on with such a work in Scandinavia: what Grieg had done for the writers of the Liberal Epoch, Sibelius was to do for literary craftsmen who are even now in labour.

Why is it that a few of the world's great men are doomed to suffer from a conspiracy of silence? They are acknowledged, howbeit taciturnly, to be great; pious genuflections are made in the direction of their work; but whenever their names crop up in conversation there is an awkward silence, as though the one who introduced them had committed an appalling social *faux pas*. If such a man is a theologian, or a politician, the reason often is that he has the reputation of a bigot; people do not speak of the Devil lest the Devil appear—to throw them in a dungeon or to pickle them in oil. How strange it is that such felonious intentions should be attributed to a musical composer! Yet possibly when the company—and critics with them—grow silent at the mention of Sibelius, it is not because they see hoof-marks on the carpet, but because they suspect a gap in their own knowledge. If so, their suspicions are correct. Forced to the point, they have written of him as a prodigy amongst barbarians; or else, flying madly from pole to pole, they have written that he was craft-brother to Tchaikovski or craft-bastard of a Strauss. The critics are never so unhappy as when they fail to fit a figure in a niche; the Plain Blunt Man is never so unhappy as when he discovers that great work is neither spectacular nor sensational.

All European countries, with the exception of Germany, are musical free-traders: their contemporary literature, on the other hand, manages seldom to scale the tariff wall. Thus countless Englishmen have listened to De Falla, never dreaming that they might read the novels of Ibanez, or to Tchaikovski while remaining unacquainted with the Russian authors. Because this free trade is in continual progress, there are many English books which breathe the spirit of Tchaikovski, and one here and there which breathes the spirit of De Falla. In the same way, there are Scandinavian books which owe each descriptive passage to the music of Sibelius; although it is unlikely that their writers have studied a single fragment from the literature of Finland.

Free trade of itself is an inadequate description, and we should not be justified in spending time on a musical influence unless there were other bonds between the traders. The Scandinavians have learnt, of course, from Beethoven and Wagner; but in neither of these cases was there a subsidiary bond. Sibelius, on the other hand, has many ties with the Scandinavian countries. Most of his ancestors were Swedish —people who lived in Finland, marrying the natives, adopting a little of the native culture, while retaining a great deal of their own. He is at home in Sweden as an Anglo-Irish squireen would have been at home in England; his language and manners are accepted; his thoughts seem sometimes foreign.

Now there were Anglo-Irish—Swift and Sheridan and

Goldsmith—who wrote better English than the English; and
Sibelius, half of Scandinavia, and half outside it, has interpreted the Scandinavian mood better than the resident composers. Where Grieg, enlarging the social drama so that it
could be understood beyond Oslo in the 'eighties, influenced
notably a single writer, Sibelius has influenced many writers,
many forms of writing, and for a longer period. And the
period has never once been static. Directly the liberals had
said to all men: "You must be free! Away with restraints!
You must be yourselves!" the men to whom they spoke
looked seriously within, wondering what this 'self' could be;
what were its possibilities, and what, if any, were its limitations.
If they had freedom, they had no notion how to use it. They
tried experiments with life: companionate marriage, homo-
sexuality, polygamy, and polyandry. No matter that these
failed, they tried equally daring experiments with art: pornography in psycho-analytical attire; sadism in pacifist attire;
cubist, surrealist, and lastly 'Realchild' drawing; music
providing the while its full quota of Rhapsodies in Blue.

Sibelius has said: "Men have mixed you cocktails of one
colour and another, but I give you nothing but cold water."
Never could a man write his autobiography in so few words,
while covering everything essential! For it was cocktails—
musical, literary, and artistic cocktails—which the majority
of twentieth-century artists gave us, once the nineteenth-
century Liberals had set them free to do so. But, if Sibelius
produced cold water—the antidote which our age was craving
—this cold water has been drawn from Finnish wells.

Because a production is unusual—that does not mean to say it
is decadent; in opposition to the life force; willing the suicide
of men. To the rest of Europe, Finland must always be unusual.
She is beyond the main grouping of our tongues; in politics
she developed suddenly, and late (one day she was a backward
region: the next she had electrified her railways and emancipated her women). She scandalizes by her detachment from an
old culture and strikes terror by her lonely knowledge of a
new one. She is Moses on Sinai, a solitary contemplative

of the future: but she is also John of the Cross or Teresa of Avila, a contemplative who has rescued all things needful from the past. Finland's conception of herself is shown to the outside world through the music of her children.

In the North a movement away from Liberalism has been a movement of the many: it has been too slow for us to notice; and it has not demanded our attention. Beginning in Finland, gathering speed in the rest of Scandinavia, the farther it progressed, the more people it found who were desiring its approach. There, as elsewhere, literature has reached a parting of the ways: one led through introspection and fruitless experiment on to cultural winter; the other through altruism on to cultural spring.

If prayer is a raising of the mind and heart to God, thought, and particularly thought expressed in art, is a releasing of energy from the mind and heart into a formless ether. Because two eyes, or two ears, are receiving-sets enough, anyone with these is able, potentially, to pick the message up. But, as a wireless station is more likely to be heard by men near than by men dwelling at a distance, so an artist's native people will be the first to feel his influence upon them. In this way, the Finns, and the Scandinavians, have worked yesterday and to-day upon the material which Sibelius could give them, while we, in our turn, may work on it to-morrow. And, just as none know what programme their neighbours have received, or whether it was more by telepathy than by direct transmission they received it, we cannot be sure that the Scandinavian writers heard this or that of Sibelius's works. Nevertheless, such a probability is almost overwhelming. To study four writers who have worked in Scandinavia since the death of Ibsen is to discover four pupils who went to the same school. The question, who was their common master, is not impossible to answer.

A good school does not produce so many exact reproductions of one type. Rather is its influence brought to bear upon a great variety of material. Finding the potential classicist, it leaves him a classic scholar; the pupil 'good at figures', and leaves him an authority on higher mathematics; the handy centre-forward, and sends him out a Soccer international. There is a mark, but it is not a trade-mark; a pattern, but it is not by any means a mould. Verner von Heidenstam does not greatly resemble Sigrid Undset—nor Selma Lagerlöf, Knut Hamsun. They received a common message, developing their individual gifts as the message prompted.

If that advanced education, which governments throughout the English-speaking world are pledged to provide for a growing number of their people, is to be, not sectional, but cultural, it must approach all manner of traditions with an open mind. The habit, nowadays, of extension-lecturers, W.E.A. tutors, and others who deal with adult classes, is to select those men and movements which they like while remaining deaf to those which are personally antipathetic. Scandinavia is one of many 'advanced' subjects which has suffered from their treatment. With passing references to Holberg, Hans Andersen, and Dalim, they have left the past of five great literary nations; concentrating wholly on the Liberal Epoch. According to this view, there was scarcely one art in Scandinavia prior to 1880, and no art at all after 1900. Some blame belongs to Shaw; but the major share must rest with those who held him to be an exponent of Scandinavian culture. Shaw's *Quintessence of Ibsenism* is out of date: because we have received worse surprises in our time, it does not shock us; because Ibsen has been answered by men of his own race, it comes as special pleading. Yet Shaw, and those who still take him for their guide, have forced a conflict, a conflict between liberalism and tradition. The suggestion here is that we shall understand it only when we see it in perspective; that all the arts should be seen together; that music is the one reliable witness in a case between different literary 'schools', since she alone is neutral.

INDEX OF PERSONS

A

Abraham, 67, 70
Albert, Prince, 11
Aldington, Richard, 98
Aquinas, St. Thomas, 43
Augustine, St., 50

B

Baum, Vicki, 117, 118
Beethoven, 132, 137
Bennett, Arnold, 88, 115
Bernanos, Georges, 71
Björnson, B., 18, 22, 25
Brandes, Georg, 26, 73, 85
Bridget, St., 16, 107
Brontë, Charlotte, 51
Browning, Robert, 103
Byrd, William, 132

C

Calvin, John, 63
Carlyle, Thomas, 123
Cartan, Shemus, *quoted*, 108
Catherine of Siena, St., 82–4
Chesterton, G. K., 17, 75, 92
Christian VIII, 62
Congar, Abbé, *quoted*, 63

D

Dante, 103
Darwin, Charles, 89, 94
De Falla, Manoel, 137
De Ternant, Philip, *quoted*, 95

Dominic, St., 28
Dostoevski, 98, 116

E

Eliot, George, 37

F

Flandin, Pierre, 103
Flaubert, Gustav, 98, 116
Forde, Parson, 79
Francis of Assisi, St., 28
Fróding, Gustaf, 77, 106

G

Galsworthy, John, 88, 114, 117
Goethe, 13
Goldsmith, Oliver, 138
Gonzaga, St. Aloysius, 72
Greene, Graham, 9
Gregory of Nyssa, St., 95–6
Grieg, Edvard H., 88, 132–6
Gunn, Neil M., *quoted*, 31

H

Hamsun, Knut, 54, 106, 114–28, 140, *quoted*, 32–3
Hardy, Thomas, 9, 39, 45, 92, 117
Harold Fairhair, 12, 16
Heidenstam, Verner von, 101–13, 140
Heiler, F., 65
Helgesen, P., 15–16
Holberg, L., 65, 140
Housman, A. E. 115

I

Ibanez, Blasco, 137
Ibsen, Henrik, 16, 20–1, 38, 43, 54, 67, 71, 73, 87, 88, 102, 135–6, 140
Ignatius of Loyola, St., 63

J

Jacobsen, J. P., 10, 87–100, 116
Joachim of Floris, 29
John of the Cross, St., 139
Joyce, James, 88

K

Kafka F., 88
Kaye-Smith, Sheila, 51
Khomiakov, *quoted*, 66
Kierkegaard, Sóren, 28, 48, 60–71, 87

L

La Fontaine, Jean de, 91
Lagerlöf, Selma, 10, 48, 72–86, 87, 106, 115, 140, *quoted*, 31–2
Lamarck, 96, 100
Laval, Pierre, 103
Lawrence, D. H., 117, 118, 119
Lenin, 43
Lie, Jonas, 21–2, 73, *quoted*, 27
Liszt, Franz, 134–5
Louis-Philippe, 61
Luther, 80

M

Maritain, Jacques, 71
Martensen, Prof., 68
Marx, Karl, 66
Mendel, Gregor, 96, 100
Mendelssohn, 132
Mill, J. S., 24, 26

Milton, John, 103
More, St. Thomas, 16
Morgan, Charles, 98
Moses, 138
Mynster, Bp., 68

N

Newman, Cardinal, 50, 62, 95
Nietzsche, 67
Nightingale, Florence, 72
Nordrák, Richard, 133

O

Olav, St., 12, 13, 84
Olsen, Regina, 70

P

Paul, St., 74
Peter, St., 47
Powys, Llewelyn, 115
Powys, Theodore, 115

Q

Quiller-Couch, Sir Arthur, 78

R

Remarque, Erich Maria, 116
Rosenberg, Alfred, 43

S

Schopenhauer, 67
Schumann, R. A., 132
Scott, Sir Walter, 37, 39, 77
Shaw, George Bernard, 65, 94, 129, 140

Sibelius, Jean, 28, 88, 110, 113, 133, 136–40
Söderblom, Bp., 65
Soloviev, S. N., 66
Sonck, Lars, 28
Spengler, Oswald, *quoted*, 67
Street, A. G., 115
Strindberg, August, 25, 73, 87, 102
Synge, John M., 15, 134

T

Tansen, 16
Tchaikovski, 137
Temple, Dr., 93
Teresa of Avila, St., 139
Thackeray, W. M., 9
Thompson, Francis, 50

U

Undset, Sigrid, 10, 15, 28, 37–59, 89, 106, 122, 140, *quoted*, 15, 33

V

Veuillot, Louis, *quoted*, 57
Voltaire, 16

W

Wagner, 67, 137
Walpole, Sir Hugh, *quoted*, 98
Watkin, E. I., *quoted*, 26
Webb, Mary, 75–6, 82, 92, 115, *quoted*, 30
Weichert, *quoted*, 117
Wells, H. G., 88, 91, 119
Wiffin, Peter, *quoted*, 30
Wilhelm II, 80

Y

Yeats, W. B., *quoted*, 15

Z

Zernov, Nicholas, 66